5/00

FRIENDS
OF ACPL

Samuel Morris

The Apostle of Simple Faith

W. Terry Whalin

CHELSEA HOUSE PUBLISHERS
Philadelphia

To my sons, Jonathan and Timothy. Like Samuel Morris, may you grow strong in your relationship with Christ.

To readers who have faced any difficulty or tragedy. May you learn from the example of Samuel Morris how to overcome any circumstance and experience the joy and love of Jesus Christ.

Cover Design: Brian Wible

First published in hardback edition © 1999 by
Chelsea House Publishers, a division of Main
Line Book Co. Printed and bound in the United
States of America.

Original paperback edition © MCMXCVI by Barbour Publishing, Inc.

1 3 5 7 9 8 6 4 2

The Chelsea House Publishers World Wide Web site
address is http:\\www.chelseahouse.com

Library of Congress Cataloging-in-Publication Data

Whalin, Terry.
    Samuel Morris / W. Terry Whalin.
    p.   cm. — (Heroes of the faith)
    Includes index.
    Summary: A biography of the son of a Kru village chief who escaped
    from his cruel captors in Liberia and who was eventually led by the
    Holy Spirit to make his way to the United States, where he in turn
    led many to God.
    ISBN 0-7910-5039-4
    1. Morris, Samuel, 1873-1893—Juvenile literature. 2. Converts—
    Liberia—Biography—Juvenile literature. 3. Christian biography—
    United States—Juvenile literature. [1. Morris, Samuel,
    1873-1893. 2. Converts. 3. Blacks—Liberia—Biography.]
    I. Title.   II. Series: Heroes of the faith (Chelsea House Publishers)
    BV4935.M63W47 1998
    270.8'1'092—dc21
    [B]   98-7108
                                                 CIP
                                                 AC

prologue

W hite puffy clouds laced the horizon. A young
African man named Samuel Morris leaned over
the railing of the ship and stared out at the
clouds. All he could see in any direction was water and
gentle waves. For almost six months, the ship had tossed
up and down sailing from Africa toward America.
The captain and crew of the ship called the young
man Sammy.

For Sammy, the voyage to America was more than a
trip. He was moving from one world into another. He got
a taste of the world ahead through the people on the ship.
Sammy was the only African in the multinational crew.

Only the day before, he had narrowly escaped death.
Their ship, loaded with rich merchant cargo, was
attacked. The men fought bravely and managed to beat
off their attackers. But some of Sammy's friends on the
ship were seriously wounded and others were killed.

His silent meditation on the water was broken with
the beginning of a small church service at sea. The captain and his crew gathered on the deck. Sammy started

the service by singing alone, "Jesus, our Shepherd, Brother, Friend, our Prophet, Priest and King, our Lord, our Life, our Way, our End, Accept the praise we bring."

After singing through this verse, Sammy stopped and asked the crewmen to join with him. During the singing, the bodies of the dead sailors were reverently lowered into the sea.

For weeks following the attack, the captain's prayer meetings were packed. The arguments and conflicts that had been so common among the crew simply disappeared during the rest of the trip to New York. Sammy was busy nursing the wounded and cleaning the ship. He didn't have time to wonder what would happen when he arrived in New York Harbor.

While in Africa, Sammy had learned about a man named Stephen Merritt. He'd decided to travel to America in order to meet Merritt and learn more about the Holy Ghost and a life that followed Jesus Christ. As the long voyage drew near the American coastline, the sailors began to question Sammy about his plans.

One of them asked, "How will you find your Stephen Merritt? Does he know you are coming?"

Another chimed in, "Sammy, do you have any idea about the size of New York City? It's huge!"

Yet another laughed, saying, "Do you think you can go into the city wearing those rags for clothes? We've got to do something about that!"

"I don't know. I don't know!" Sammy cried. "But my heavenly Father knows, and He will show me. Didn't He bring me to New York?" The crew nodded and had to admit defeat. They could see the determination in Sammy's eyes. There was no deterring this young man.

"At least we can give him some clothes," the German crewman decided. Harold contributed a pair of cut-off green pants. The Malay who had once plotted to kill Sammy wanted to give the young African a red great-coat, but everyone laughed at the idea. "He can't walk around in that heavy thing," someone said.

Finally, the crew located a light jacket and a shirt with short sleeves. "It will have to do," the German said with a sigh. "At least Sammy has a decent hat and good shoes." No one was concerned that the shoes for Sammy were three sizes larger than necessary.

Suddenly the captain shouted, "Oh, Sammy come and see!" The captain pointed toward the distant shore. Sammy could see a statue of a woman holding a large torch. The captain explained, "The Statue of Liberty is a symbol of hope for the poor."

"What does it mean?" Sammy asked looking at the huge figure.

"It means you are welcome to America, Samuel Morris. See how new that statue looks? The Statue of Liberty has only been here a few years. Now you can do whatever you wish in America."

"I wish to see Stephen Merritt and learn about the Holy Ghost," the boy said with determination.

"Then you are free to do so," the captain assured Sammy with a hug. Many of the crew had lumps in their throats and tears in their eyes as they overheard the words.

"There it is, Sammy," pointed one of the sailors.

"New York!"

Sammy's face lit up with excitement—New York. At long last, after almost six months at sea, he had reached his destination. The buildings of the city rose above the harbor like a bustling crowd. Sammy had never before seen so many buildings at one place.

The late afternoon sun cast a golden hue over the city. The water rushed smoothly toward the dock, lapping its sides and breaking away again with swaying rhythm.

"Well, we made it!" boomed the captain's voice. "And what a lovely Friday is it, too!" He smiled at Sammy. "You certainly earned your pay."

Tears fell from Sammy's eyes. It had been a Friday when the voice had urged him to run from the Grebos. It had been a Friday when he had reached the settlement near Monrovia. And now he had arrived in New York on the same day.

"My emancipation day!" he cried joyfully. He turned his face toward heaven. "I thank You for this day, Father. I will ever dedicate Fridays to you. I will neither eat nor drink on this day, but will hunger and thirst after You."

Captain and crew alike tearfully bade good-bye to the boy who had shown them the way of love. The boundaries of each race had melted before the power of God's love. They would never forget Sammy Morris. Sammy Morris hoped they would never forget the One who had kept them all in His care.

That Friday in September 1891, Sammy ventured down the gangplank. He walked along the wharf on the East River with one goal in his mind. *Find Stephen*

Merritt. No one paid any attention to the oddly dressed black boy. He was so intent on his mission that he hardly noticed the streets or buildings. Finally, he saw a man who was as ill-dressed as he was. This man didn't seem to be going anywhere.

"Excuse me, sir," said Sammy. "Can you tell me where I can find Stephen Merritt?"

Out of the hundreds of people who could have been walking by, this person was a homeless man who had often found help and food at Stephen Merritt's mission.

"Well, this is Pike Street," responded the man. "Mr. Merritt's way over on Eighth Avenue. That's three or four miles from here." He studied the young man from Africa. "I'll take you to him for a dollar," he said, scenting a profit.

"All right," said Sammy. Sammy did not have a dollar. In fact, he didn't have any money, but he knew his heavenly Father would provide. Before he left Africa, the Reverend C. E. Smirl told Sammy that he'd need one hundred dollars to reach America. While Sammy never received one hundred dollars, he had arrived in America. Because the Lord had provided passage to the United States, He would provide the dollar this man demanded. Sammy went with the man in confidence and faith.

The man led Sammy along many streets full of hurrying people. Sammy's eyes filled with wonder at the sight of crowds and buildings. His ears rang with the sounds of carriage wheels rolling on the street and horses braying while drivers called out instructions.

There were many kinds of noises. The smells were

the most overpowering. Garbage was thrown into the streets, and the strong odor of garlic and smothering sooty air assailed Sammy's nose.

"The sailors told me this was such a wonderful place," he kept reminding himself. "Why is everyone in such a hurry?" The man led Sammy up and down the streets of New York. They reached Eighth Avenue and arrived at their destination just as Stephen Merritt was slipping his key into the lock of his office door.

"See the man unlocking his door?" Sammy's guide asked him. "That is Stephen Merritt, the man who is putting his key into his pocket."

Sammy hurried up to the stranger. "Stephen Merritt?"

"Yes," replied Mr. Merritt.

"I am Sammy Morris," said the boy. "I have just come from Africa to talk to you about the Holy Ghost."

Merritt regarded the young black man with surprise, then smiled and asked, "Do you have any letters of introduction from your church leaders?"

"No. I did not have time to wait," responded Sammy. "I came as fast as I could."

Stephen Merritt smiled at the eagerness in the boy's face and words. "I have to go over to Jane Street just now for a prayer meeting. You go into our mission next door here and wait for me. Make yourself at home. When I return, we'll see what we can do for you." There was something in the boy's eyes that interested Mr. Merritt.

Sammy nodded in agreement. "All right, Stephen Merritt." As Samuel moved toward the door of the mission, his entrepreneurial guide suddenly called out, "Hey, what about my dollar?"

Sammy waved in the direction of Mr. Merritt. "Oh, Stephen Merritt pays all my bills now," responded Sammy with confidence.

Mr. Merritt smiled at his new student as he handed the dollar to the homeless man and then climbed into his coach. *Well, what will we do with this one?* he asked himself.

Sammy nodded his appreciation. Then he walked inside the mission. Unkempt men lined the walls of the plain room. When Sammy stood beside one of the men, he was motioned to the rear of the line. "Don't ever try to break into line," the beggar in front of him explained. "These guys don't mess around. They wouldn't mind smacking you."

As the line moved forward, Sammy moved, too. Soon he saw that each man received a bowl of soup and a piece of bread. After his long walk to the mission, it felt good to take his soup to an empty chair and sit down for a bit.

"Yeah, there's only one problem with taking this soup," grumbled the man beside Samuel. "They expect you to stay for the preaching."

"Are we having preaching?" Sammy asked as he looked around the room. It was a square, plain room, but he noticed a pulpit on the far wall. It reminded him of his mission back in Africa, only the audience was quite different. These men looked even worse than the sailors on the ship. All eighteen men gave off strong odors from not washing. No one seemed to mind except Sammy.

As each man finished eating, they took their spoon and bowl into the kitchen, where a rosy-faced woman was washing dishes. Then the men sat in rows of chairs facing the pulpit. Sammy followed the example of the others.

Soon the meeting started. Sammy was delighted that they sang hymns he knew. His voice filled the small room. Then a young man stepped to the pulpit, looking a bit uncertain. He explained that this was his first sermon. Some of the audience sneered.

Sammy recalled the first time that he had spoken in public and felt very sympathetic toward the young man. The preacher had prepared several pages for his message, but it didn't take him long to read through it. Because he had not used all of his time, the preacher asked for testimonies.

Sammy was the first person to stand up. He walked to the pulpit as he had learned at the mission in Africa. In an English accent strange to the ears of the men in the room, Sammy began to tell of his beatings as a youth, his time with the missionaries, his five-month sea voyage to America.

Suddenly the heads that had been drooping in the crowd began to take great interest in what Sammy was saying. Every man was electrified from God's working in the young African's life.

At the end of his message, Sammy said, "Let's pray." He knelt on the floor and lifted his hands in the air. He refused to begin praying until every man in the room was also kneeling in a circle around him. Then he prayed and begged the men to join in.

Gradually some of the men prayed aloud. Some whispered their prayers with Samuel crying aloud to God.

Several hours later, Stephen Merritt returned to the mission. He remembered his promise to join Sammy. He returned to one of the great surprises of his life. He found Sammy kneeling on the platform of the mission, surrounded by seventeen men on their faces. They were weeping and praying in repentance.

Merritt was stunned. This young man, who virtually had no education or training and who came from what was then considered a "heathen" continent, had led nearly twenty people to Christ on his first night in America! Stephen Merritt recognized immediately that Sammy Morris had been empowered and sent to the United States by the Lord. He knelt and prayed with the men.

At the end of their prayer time, the student preacher began a song, and everyone sang praises to God. The Spirit of God touched hearts. That evening marked the beginning of Samuel Morris's ministry in America, but it did not mark the beginning of his walk with God. That had happened years earlier when he was known as Prince Kaboo, son of the Kru village's chief. As the pages of this book will tell, Samuel Morris had taken a long journey to do so much for God.

one

Margol jumped at the sudden noise behind him. Startled, he turned to the young man and snapped, "Why do you scare me?"

"Margol, you scare too easily. I didn't mean to scare you. I only want to know what you are doing."

Margol met Prince Kaboo's questioning eyes. Looking ashamed, he answered, "I'm making an altar."

"*Haw-wu!* What for?" Prince Kaboo watched as Margol whittled a stick for the altar.

"I pray and leave food for the living dead. I want them to help me," Margol said as he pointed to himself. "The Grebos might come back, and the living dead can protect us."

Both Prince Kaboo and Margol couldn't imagine any greater danger than the Grebos. The Grebo people were known for their fierce fighting and the horrible things they did to their enemies. After conquering a village, they would set fire to everything in it.

"Margol, do you really think an altar will keep the Grebos away?" Prince Kaboo shook his head at the idea.

"It certainly can't hurt anything," Margol said as he returned to his work. He searched for a three-forked branch to hold a small bowl. Once he had it secured, the boys gazed upward. "This branch will hold my bowl more securely," Margol predicted.

"Not an empty bowl, I hope," Kaboo said.

"No. I told you a few minutes ago that I will keep this bowl filled with food for the living dead," Margol said.

"*Haw-wu!* What boasting about this bowl! You will forget and eat all of the food yourself."

"Don't be so sure, silly boy. You don't remember that my grandmother died the last moon. She watches me every minute, and I will not forget her. She will eat this food."

"So you think your grandmother is one of the living dead?" Kaboo asked his friend.

"Yes," Margol answered firmly. "She may be invisible, but that doesn't mean she and other ancestors aren't watching over what I do."

Prince Kaboo stood quietly for a long time and then decided to make an altar as well. After discarding several wooden blocks because of various flaws, Kaboo found a block that would work well and began to carve it.

"Ah! You're making it too big," Margol said.

"It's better for it to be bigger," Prince Kaboo said. "Then I can feed more of the living dead. We will need all the protection we can get if the Grebos come back. I heard my father say they will."

"It must be nice to be the chief's son and hear all of the important men talk," Margol declared.

"Father seldom lets me listen," Prince Kaboo responded as he continued digging wood from the center of his bowl.

Margol ran off to find kola beans for his bowl. When he returned, he filled the bowl with beans, seeds, a lizard, and three snails. Satisfied with his completed task, Margol sat under the shade of a mango tree and watched Prince Kaboo continue to work on his altar. They were on the edge of the mango trees near their Kru village. It was harvest season, and the grove of trees vibrated with movement and sounds.

Margol and Kaboo were members of the Kru tribe, which lived somewhere between the river Sestas and Grand Sisters in the forests of Liberia, West Africa. Liberia got its name from the Latin word for liberty. It was given that name when the nation became the home for slaves who were freed when slavery was abolished in America. Many liberated slaves who wished to return to Africa settled in Liberia. They set up their capital city in Monrovia and lived mostly on the strip of land along the coast.

These former slaves had been in contact with Europeans and Americans, and many of them were Christians. Their lifestyle was quite different from that of the people who lived in the interior of Liberia. Thousands of people like Kaboo and Margol had never seen a non-African and had never heard the name of Jesus.

Kaboo was born about 1873, although his people did not keep written records of births. Kaboo's father was a chief among the Kru people. They were tall people for that area of Africa, and they mostly hunted and fished.

The Grebos and the Kru people had been fighting for years. Sometimes the disputes between the two groups would linger for weeks. Years before Kaboo was born, there had been a dispute over some farming land. For a long time the quarrel dragged on, and then the Grebos invited the Krus to send some of their leaders to discuss terms of peace.

Twenty-eight Krus went to the conference and were welcomed with signs of great friendliness. A bull was killed and large quantities of rice and red peppers were prepared for the feast. After everyone had eaten their fill, the men sat down in a large hut to begin the discussion. Then the women and children who had watched the feast were allowed to eat the leftover food.

Some of the men were squatting. Others were sitting on blocks of wood, broad poles, or stones. Suddenly a shrill whistle pierced the air. The Grebo warriors who gathered outside the hut burst in and attacked the Krus with knives, clubs, and spears. For a few minutes, everything was confusion. The air was filled with the noise of battle and with cries of pain and anger.

The Krus were unarmed and outnumbered. They had no chance against their fierce attackers. Two of them frantically tore holes in the grass walls of the hut and managed to escape. The remaining twenty-six were brutally murdered.

The two men who escaped made off into the bush. One of them became Chief Kaboo, Prince Kaboo's father. Kaboo was a family name used by all the male members of the family.

When Prince Kaboo was born, the Kru people had a great celebration. The fact that Kaboo lived was unusual because four out of five children in his village died in infancy. In the eyes of the people, a baby boy showed great favor from the gods. Soon after his birth, the baby was forced to endure a cold bath, intended to make him strong. His tender body was rubbed with salt or red peppers.

When Kaboo was only a few days old, rice, leaves, corn, palm butter, and chunks of meat were crammed down his throat. The Kru believed these foods were strong man's food and that eating them would make the child strong.

After it was clear that Kaboo had survived the ordeal —and many Kru babies did not—his body was rubbed with sand and coconut bark to toughen him. Apart from his mother's milk, he would never have another drop of milk. His diet included elephant and monkey meat and an occasional bush rat. As Prince Kaboo grew older, he learned to play a variety of games. He was taught to hurl a stone with a sling and to shoot an arrow from a bow.

But the Kru village continued to be raided by the Grebos. After each raid, villagers struggled to rebuild and often had only bush rats, snails, and slugs to eat. When they could, they killed a hippopotamus—or bush cow, as they called them—to supplement their diet. Fear of another assault by the Grebos motivated Kaboo and his friend to build their altar to the living dead.

"It looks like you will never finish. Let me help," Margol offered.

"Help indeed! With luck, I will finish before the sun dips below the ground."

"Luck you say. You'd better move your hands like the bird's wings," Margol taunted.

"Just you watch. When the sun dips low, my altar will be finished," Prince Kaboo said with resolve in his voice.

"I'll get the food. It will take many snails to fill that big bowl."

Margol slipped away into the jungle to search for the snail offering. In many ways, these two boys were like a couple of beans in a kola pod. They were close friends and did almost everything together. Neither boy wore shoes to protect his feet from the deadly throes of the jungles and the burning sands of the tropics. Also they wore little clothing to protect their black skin from the strong sun.

Margol returned as the sun was setting. The prince had finished his carving and placed his bowl in the mango tree near Margol's altar.

"Wow!" Margol admitted. "You weren't boasting when you said you would finish the bowl today."

"It was a difficult promise to keep," Kaboo confessed. "My hands ache."

Margol put the food safely inside Kaboo's bowl. "Ah! Now the living dead will watch for us and protect us."

They can't hurt anything, Kaboo thought, *but they probably won't help us.* The prince wanted to believe that the living dead would keep his village from harm. At the same time, he remembered the last raid from the Grebo people. Many Kru warriors had been killed or captured. Now that the Kru village had so few warriors left, the prince wondered what would happen when they were attacked again.

Only a few days later, Prince Kaboo learned the answer to his questions about the village's protection. As the sun crept over the edge of the horizon, he heard the cry, "Grebos!"

Screams filled the air as flaming arrows fell on the round straw huts. Prince Kaboo knew exactly what to do. He had been taught to run. Amid the clattering and clanging of flashing spears, the young prince wasted no time. With the other children, he splashed across the river and climbed a tall tree.

As he clung to a high branch in the tree, the prince watched the women help little children across the murky-colored river. The Grebos circled the village, throwing their flaming spears. Prince Kaboo snorted, "Worthless goats! Worthless goats!"

As he continued watching, Kaboo saw Kru warriors shoot arrows, shout orders, and beat the flames until the fire finally forced them outside the village. One by one the warriors were killed or captured. Prince Kaboo trembled with rage. He felt completely helpless watching the Grebos steal the cattle, rob the villagers' huts, and carry away the stores of rice.

As the Kru warriors wailed, the prince covered his face and moaned, "Oh, look at the blood! If only I could do something." But there was nothing for him to do. His job was to survive.

After the Grebo tribe took their captives and plunder

away, Prince Kaboo climbed down the tree and hurried across the river. Some parts of the village continued to smolder and burn. The prince stamped out the sputtering remains of the fire. He stared at the pile of cinders that had been the chief's hut. Swaying and shuffling, he wandered over the well-trodden ground calling out, "Father! Mother!"

His eyes focused on the mango tree where he had placed his bowl to the living dead. The branches were burned and the altar was black, but the charred food remained. The prince stared in silence at the altar for a long time. Then he said bitterly, "So, this is how you protect me."

Prince Kaboo huddled against a tree with his head down and his shoulders hunched. It was there that his father, the chief, found him. "Come now, Son. Your mother will worry about you. Your sister is safe, but Margol is dead."

The prince began to wail. Suddenly he turned and looked back at Margol's altar. "He thought you would protect him!" Kaboo screamed at the living dead who had failed him.

Slowly, he joined the other Kru people who were creeping back to the charred remains of their village. Chief Kaboo tightly hugged his little prince and took him to where Kaboo's mother and his little sister, Yout, were waiting for them.

Mother had remained on the other side of the river until every little child had safely crossed the river and returned to what was left of the village. The four members of Kaboo's family cleaned up the burned straw where their hut had been and struggled to build another shelter.

Almost everyone in the village had lost a family member. With sad faces and feelings, the people scratched through the ruins looking for food. One thing was plentiful: palm branches for building new huts. The Grebos had ruined their gardens and stolen most of their animals and rice, but they had left plenty of palms.

The Kru people managed to stay alive by eating roots, raw monkeys, and coconuts. No other food was available until they could harvest new gardens and start new herds.

As Prince Kaboo grew older, the village grew stronger, but the children remembered the vicious attack that had cost them so much. They were filled with hatred for the Grebos.

One of the Kru ways to get revenge was to chant against the Grebos. Prince Kaboo and other young people spent long hours dancing and chanting against the Grebos. Word spread that the young men were planning revenge. Though they had been children during the last raid, they now considered themselves the warriors of the tribe.

"My son!"

Kaboo looked up in surprise. "Yes, my father?" While Kaboo was only about fifteen, he had spent a great deal of time with his father—even more than the Head Counselor. After all, the chief was proud to have his eldest son, the prince, at his side.

"Listen! What am I hearing?"

Kaboo lifted his head and held his breath for several seconds. He could hear nothing. Nothing, that is except for the low conversation of people in the compound huts as they began to wake up early in the morning. What else could it be?

"I hear nothing, my father."

"Quiet! Everyone of you!" the older man commanded the villagers who stood nearby. Something was definitely wrong for the chief to speak in that tone of voice. He never spoke sharply. He was the chief of that village, and whatever he said, the people obeyed.

The sudden silence played loudly in Kaboo's ears.

A sound rolled toward them on the wind. It grew louder until no one could doubt where it came from.

"The drums!" they whispered. "What are they saying?"

The deep voice of the talking drums sounded louder. No one could mistake the message, "The enemy is here!"

Immediately the village sprang into action and noise. Young men ran for their spears and sharpened their knives. The women forgot about their food preparations, rushing instead to get the small children to safety. Everyone was preparing for the coming battle, but because many of them had been asleep, they were not ready when their enemies arrived.

The Grebos had decided to stir up the other tribes and villages against the Kru. The Grebos told the other villages that Chief Kaboo was planning to conquer all the other people along the coast. All the tribes banded together with the Grebos to attack the Kru.

The sunrise attack was all too successful. Fight as they

21

might, there was no way the Kru could defend themselves against such a large force. At the end of the day, the sun dipped quickly behind the horizon, as if to shield its face from the blood and dead bodies.

Most of the Kru people turned away from the ceremony that marked their defeat. They could not bear to watch the proud chief and father of Prince Kaboo be humiliated. The old chief put his face on the ground before the cruel Grebo chief who had defeated him.

With deep sorrow, the Kru chief said, "Yes, all you ask I will do. See we have given you everything from our village. We will gather the rest and bring it to you on the day that you select. Your words are good."

"We will take your son until you bring the rest of the goods," answered the cruel chief.

"Ah, I beg you—don't take my son. We will do everything that you ask. You can trust us. Only leave me my son!"

"He is ours," the Grebo chief shouted with anger.

At those words, Kaboo felt sick with fear. He knew the terrible reality of captivity as a pawn or captive. Already, Kaboo had suffered twice as a pawn to other chiefs.

Roughly the enemy seized Kaboo and tied his hands. Soon the loads were ready, and off they started to a camp some miles from their village. Kaboo looked back sadly at his people. Tears came to his eyes at the great sorrow on the face of his father.

"Do not be afraid for me, Father. It will not be long," Kaboo cried. "You will get the goods soon, and I shall be back before too long."

It was the last time he would see his village home.

The hot African sun poured down on the clearing where Prince Kaboo stood, surrounded by Grebo men and boys. Kaboo's father and his people had brought the first payment toward buying back their prince. They had labored hard to gather baskets of palm kernels, chunks of dried rubber, and a few pieces of ivory to place at the feet of their enemy. To their dismay, the Grebo chief shook his head and laughed at their offering.

The Grebo chief taunted Kaboo. His father, Chief Kaboo, glared at the chief of the Grebo tribe. The boy met the gaze of his enemy with steady eyes, but his young heart pounded with fear and dread. *Oh, please, Father*, he thought. *Please rescue me.*

Chief Kaboo looked down at his namesake. He placed a hand upon the boy's shoulder. "I will buy you back, Kaboo. You'll see. As soon as we are able, we will buy you back."

The chief of the Grebo people stepped forward, his eyes hungry with greed. "You know the terms of our agreement. Every new moon, you must bring us the tribute that you owe us. Make sure you come with full payment. If you fail to pay, it won't go very well for your prince." His harsh laughter filled Kaboo's ears. "Your prince is now a pawn. Again!"

"We will pay!" countered the chief of the Kru tribe. "We will pay." His words were tinged with anger.

"Take him away!" commanded the triumphant

23

African chief. He signaled to one of his warriors. The warrior stepped forward and took the young boy by the arm. As Kaboo was led away, the warriors whooped and laughed in triumph.

Kaboo looked back and saw his father standing in the clearing. The young boy's eyes pleaded for help. If only his father could reach out and rescue him! If only his father could take him by the arm and bring him home!

The Kru chief signaled to his son to be brave. The boy was pushed forward. With a heavy heart he walked away, the distance between his father and himself widening with every step. The warriors and their prize pawn disappeared into the lush foliage of the jungle.

The plaintive call of a dove mirrored the harsh loneliness that flooded the heart of the young prisoner. Would he ever see his father again? Would he ever be free from this terrible cycle of suffering?

The victorious Grebo tribe demanded payment to insure peace. And until the Kru could make payment in full, Kaboo knew he would continue to be held as a pawn. Kaboo walked the trail to the Grebo camp. The warriors prodded him with their spears. With every jab, his body shivered with fear. He already knew the cruelty that awaited him. The cold heart of the Grebo chief allowed for no mercy toward any slave, especially for the pawned prince.

Despite his fears, the young boy held his head high. *I must be brave*, he told himself. *I must be brave for my father. He will buy me back. I know he will.*

At the camp, Kaboo was thrown into a hut where the

other slaves were imprisoned. They greeted him in silence, their eyes void of hope. Kaboo closed his eyes and tried to sleep. Outside, the Grebos celebrated the anniversary of their victory with feasting, drinking, and dancing. The rhythm of the drums beat loudly in the ears of Prince Kaboo, drowning out the pounding of his lonely heart.

When the next payment day arrived, Kaboo's father came with all the ivory, rubber, kola nuts, and other goods his people had managed to collect. The cruel Grebo chief examined all of the items.

"It is not enough!" scoffed the Grebo chief. "You must bring me more!"

Kaboo's father was almost in despair over the reaction. "I will bring more," he said, "only release my son so he can return with me."

"He will not be freed," the victorious chief replied. "You insult me with this meager payment. Can it be that you are too lazy to work for the young prince?" He pointed to Kaboo, who stood at the edge of the clearing, two warriors on either side of him.

Kaboo's hopes for freedom crumpled beneath the scornful laughter of the Grebo chief. The boy stood straight and tall, despite the weariness with which his muscles ached. The Grebos forced Kaboo to work from the first trace of dawn until darkness fell. But for his father's sake and for the honor of his tribe, Kaboo would let no sign of strain betray his tiredness or his fears.

25

The chief of the Kru looked at his son, his eyes filled with longing. He knew many new moons would come and go before he would be able to pay off the Grebos.

"I am weary of your presence," snapped the Grebo chief. "Go back to your camp." His dark eyes glistened in the afternoon sun. "See to it that your people work harder," he hissed. "Perhaps I shall have to provide you with some incentive." He threw back his head and laughed. His warriors brandished their spears at Kaboo and joined their voices with the laughter of their chief.

Chief Kaboo turned away, signaling his men to follow. Once again young Kaboo felt the pain of separation tear at his heart. The bonds of slavery tightened around his mind, freezing all thought of freedom.

Suddenly, the drums in the camps began to beat slowly, with a taunting rhythm. Kaboo's blood ran cold. He watched as the chief gave a signal to his men. The other slaves were brought into the clearing. One of the guards grabbed Kaboo and led him to a tree at the edge of the camp. Using a rough, thick piece of vine, they quickly tied the young prince to the tree.

The Grebo chief drank deeply from a nearby pot of rum. He laughed long and hard. The drums beat faster. Grabbing a thorny vine from the hands of an assistant, the chief leaned down to whisper in his captive's ear, "I hope this will inspire your father to pay us in full." He waved the vine in front of Kaboo's face.

The young boy gritted his teeth. *Be brave*, he said to himself. *Be brave.*

The chief laughed again and nodded to the drummers.

26

The hands of the drummers became a blur and the rhythm reached a feverish pitch.

The chief raised the thick vine over his head and let out a piercing scream. With all his might, he brought down the whip across the young boy's soft ebony back. The poisonous thorns tore open Kaboo's flesh in streaks of pain. Again and again, the chief whipped the boy. Each lashing was more prolonged and severe than the one before it. Each stroke tore into Kaboo's flesh and implanted a fiery virus. Before long Kaboo felt like his entire body was on fire.

The Grebos laughed and shrieked at the sight of their pawn's torture. They danced around the camp, mimicking the beating, pulling down imaginary whips, and screaming gleefully.

Kaboo endured the pain as best he could. He fought the urge to scream. The intense pain forced involuntary tears to slip silently down his cheeks.

Finally the chief held the whip still. He turned to the horrified Kru slaves who had been forced to watch their prince's torture. He pointed to one of the slaves. The young woman was pushed forward. She stood trembling before the dreaded chief.

"Go back to your camp. Tell Chief Kaboo and your people what you have seen with your own eyes." He flicked the vine toward the bleeding pawn. "This is how your prince will be treated until you pay his ransom in full. Now go!" he commanded.

The woman dashed out of the camp and disappeared down the trail. Kaboo was untied and secured inside the prisoner's hut. His back burned with pain. The poison from the thorns infected his blood, causing chills and fever. For the moment, the terrible physical pain crowded out the agony of his tortured soul. He fell into a troubled sleep.

The noisy chatter of the pepper bird greeted the rising sun and awakened Kaboo from his sleep. He shifted painfully to his side. The open cuts on his back and legs were caked with dried blood. Fiery red tentacles of infection crisscrossed his skin. Breathing burned his chest. But pain was no excuse. Work must still be done.

When Chief Kaboo returned home, he asked his people to give up the last things that they had. Each month the Krus were to give the Grebos their ivory, palm nuts, and India rubber. As each new moon arrived, the Kru brought everything that they could give, but the Grebos always said it was not enough for the life of a prince. The cruel Grebo chief grew angry. "Is this all you bring me?" he taunted. "You must bring much more."

"We have no more; that is all there is," Kaboo's father replied. A great fear came over him. He knew now they would never be able to pay enough. He feared that his son could not live much longer under the cruel beatings.

The boy trailed his finger slowly in the dusty smoothness of the hard-packed dirt floor. Several new moons had come and gone. With each passing month, Kaboo's

28

hopes for freedom had dwindled. The offerings his father presented to the greedy Grebo chief were never satisfactory.

With each failed visit, the enemy chief poured out his wrath on young Kaboo. The flesh of his back hung in shreds. His body was covered with open sores and burns from the whippings. He was exhausted from loss of blood and fever.

Kaboo sighed. He was kept isolated from the other slaves. The loneliness and lack of love was more than he could bear. The customary lucky charms of his people that he wore around his neck and ankles had long since been stripped from him. They had not protected him from harm, anyway. His body was gravely weakened by what had become daily torture.

Still the Grebos forced the young prince to work. Kaboo was angry and desperate. *I must do something*, he thought. He decided to try an escape. It was his only hope.

A sudden commotion in the camp pulled Kaboo's head from the floor. Dogs barked wildly. Young children shouted and jeered the visitors.

"Father," whispered Kaboo.

Two warriors burst into Kaboo's hut. They jerked him roughly to his feet. Kaboo was escorted to the center of the clearing. His heart raced at seeing the face of his father.

In the clearing, Chief Kaboo and his people placed baskets of rice at the feet of the Grebo chief. The harvest had been plentiful. Surely this time it was enough! Kaboo

29

looked eagerly to watch the response of the Grebo chief.

"You must be joking," snarled the chief. He reached out with his foot and kicked one of the baskets over. "This is hardly a tribute worthy of such a great and mighty warrior as I!"

The Grebos shouted in agreement with their chief. Kaboo's father stepped forward and stared determinedly into his enemy's eyes.

"I assumed you were going to respond unfavorably to our generous offering," he said boldly. "Therefore I have another offer to make."

The Grebo chief leaned forward, his eyes glinting with greed.

"What is it?" he demanded.

Chief Kaboo signaled to one of the Kru. One of the women came forth from the group, leading a little girl by the hand. Kaboo sucked in his breath.

Yout! Kaboo stared with longing at his sister. The sight of her chubby cheeks and sweet brown eyes overwhelmed Kaboo with feelings of love and longing. The little girl looked around the camp, bewildered. She was too frightened to cry.

"This is my daughter," Chief Kaboo announced. "Take her as a pawn and give me back my son. We will then pay the balance of the ransom as soon as we can."

The Grebo chief shook his head in disbelief. "Your daughter? You are offering me a worthless female child?"

He threw back his head and began to laugh. His cruel laughter slapped across Kaboo's heart like a whip.

"You must take my daughter!" insisted Chief Kaboo.

"My people need their prince. You have kept him long enough. Be reasonable."

To the surprise of everyone, young Kaboo stepped forward.

"No, Father. No," begged Kaboo. "Do not do this thing. I am a prince. I can bear this torture much better than my sister could. Please, do not offer her. I am strong. I can do it."

All eyes were on young Kaboo. His father looked at his son, his heart breaking at the sight of his brave young face.

"That's very noble of you," jeered the Grebo chief, "but I would never accept this ridiculous offer." He turned his attention to Kaboo's father. "Your daughter has no worth! You are desperate! Only cowards and fools wear their desperation on their faces. Get out! And next month you had better not fail to please me." He looked menacingly at his pawn. "You had better not fail," he repeated.

Kaboo's father turned away. One of the women picked up Yout and followed quickly after her people. Young Kaboo was dragged to the field to work. By noon, the chief was drunk, his anger over the latest offer fueled by the rum. He ordered Kaboo brought to the whipping tree. The boy was beaten until he passed out. Another Kru slave was released.

"Tell your chief that's what I think about his stupid offer!" shouted the chief after the fleeing slave. His words were slurred. "Tell him his precious son is paying for his father's foolishness."

31

When Kaboo came to, he found himself on the ground of the hut. His strength had drained away. Bleeding and infection were drawing the life from his young body. All hope drained from him as he lay on the floor.

I'm going to die, he thought. He remembered what he had been taught about the spirits that lived in the water and trees and stones. They had not helped him to escape his suffering. Thoughts of death terrified him.

What happens to you when you die? the boy wondered. In his short life, he had seen a lot of death. Young children and old people dying from illness, young men killed by their enemies. It was always the same. Life disappeared. The person was cut off from those who knew him. Was there only endless darkness after death? Did death stretch on forever like a black river of separation and nothingness?

When the next new moon arrived, Kaboo's father did not appear. When it became obvious to the Grebos that Kaboo's father was not going to return again, the angry chief ordered Kaboo to be beaten every day. Each beating was longer and harder than the one before it.

Because of the poisonous vine they used for a whip, each stroke tore open his back and caused him great pain. The poor boy felt as though his whole body was on fire. Each time Kaboo was beaten, another Kru slave watched and then was sent to Kaboo's father with the horrible tale of the whipping.

"It will be much worse for the prince if you do not

pay at all," the chief warned. But nothing could be done. There was no more for the Kru people to give to the Grebos.

Kaboo's wounds did not have time to heal from the beatings. The flesh on his back was cut to pieces again and again. Kaboo knew that his only hope was escape, but what hope did a half-dead boy who was watched constantly have of running away?

One day Kaboo was beaten in the sight of all the camp and his neck was placed in a stock made of two wooden beams that closed over his neck. His head stuck out from the hole. Then the Grebos left him alone to suffer. Kaboo saw blood oozing from his wounds, and fear gripped him. "I must escape or I die," he gasped.

He hoped he would die before he met the awful death his enemies were preparing for him. They were digging a large hole in the ground where they were going to put Kaboo if his father did not return.

There he would be buried up to his neck, then they would hold his mouth open with a stick, and honey would be rubbed on his face to draw the ants from a nearby anthill. The terrible driver ants would then come and eat up his body bit by bit. After the driver ants had taken away every bit of his flesh, his enemies would put his bones in front of his hut as a warning to others who did not pay their debts.

The prince strained to push the two beams apart. To his surprise, one beam moved. With his hands, he forced the loose beam away from his neck, but he could not escape.

The next two days blended into a painful blur of

fierce whippings. Soon he became so weak from fever and loss of blood that he could not even stand or sit up. Two logs were tied together to form a crosstree. Kaboo was thrown over the crosstree, and his bleeding back was beaten again.

Kaboo was dying. The fear of death no longer mattered. He only wanted release from the relentless suffering. It was late afternoon, a Friday. A sliver of the moon hung over the jungle, anticipating the night. Kaboo heard the sound of digging. He lifted his head as best he could from where he hung over the cross of wood. His captors continued digging the deep hole.

When the men finished, they leaned over Kaboo.

"Unless your father comes back with your ransom, we will bury you alive!" They pointed to the hole. "Say hello to your grave, Kru boy." They walked away to summon the chief.

The chief surveyed the hole and declared it sufficient. He signaled for another slave to be brought out to witness another beating of the pawn. A young Kru boy was led out to the clearing to watch the terrible display.

Kaboo stared blankly into space, his body crying out for relief from the unending agony of pain. Thoughts of his father and sister swirled vaguely in his mind. Nothing mattered anymore.

Suddenly, a bright light like a flash of lightening shone out over Kaboo and his wooden cross. "Aiiee!" yelped the terrified Grebo chief and his men. The light blinded their eyes. They were stunned, helpless. The young Kru slave brought out to witness the torture of his prince watched the fantastic scene with amazement.

Kaboo heard a loud voice that seemed to be coming from above him. The voice commanded, "Rise up, Kaboo! Rise up and run away!"

Instantly, the ropes that bound Kaboo fell from his hands. Strength surged through his body. Throughout that day, he had had nothing to eat or drink, yet he felt neither hunger nor thirst nor weakness. Jumping up, Kaboo obeyed the wonderful voice and ran away from the surprised Africans as fast as a deer. While the Grebos stumbled helplessly around the camp, Kaboo disappeared into the jungle.

Kaboo had no idea where the strange voice and light had come from. He had never heard of the Christian God. He knew nothing of God's help nor had he heard of Jesus Christ, who had once been a pawn like himself.

The earthly prince who had hung on a crosstree did not know that there was once a heavenly Prince named Jesus, who had been beaten and killed on another tree— a cross on the hill of Calvary. No one had told him that this heavenly Prince rose from the dead and is living today to bring life and help to others.

The only thing that Kaboo knew was that a strange and unseen power had come to his assistance. Swiftly, Kaboo ran into the forest.

Don't take the path, he told himself and stumbled into the bush. He squirmed between roots and scratched his way through the tall brush. Poisonous cobras, lizards, and vipers lay in wait, but Kaboo didn't fear them as much as he feared being returned to the Grebos.

35

As Kaboo tried to decide where to go, he rubbed his eyes. To his utter amazement the light that had burst upon him in the Grebo camp was still with him! With the help of that light, Kaboo journeyed on through the jungle. He was able to find fruit, nuts, and roots to eat. He ran like the wind. The prince was surefooted, guided by the light.

Night fell quickly, blanketing the jungle completely with darkness. Countless insects and tree frogs wove a cloth of endless music for the night to wear. As he ran, the boy marveled at what had happened. What was this strange light? Whose voice and helping hand had reached out and set him free? The answers to his questions would have to wait. For the moment, he must put as much distance between himself and his enemies as was possible.

Not knowing where he was going, Kaboo traveled on. He slowed his run only when he felt confident that his enemies could not catch up to him for the moment. A dead teak tree loomed in the shadows. Kaboo searched it with his hands and discovered the trunk was hollow. He slipped inside the tree. He could sleep safely there.

The black of night was softening into the gray of dawn. Kaboo stayed in the tree. It would be too risky to travel during the day. He feared being seen by anyone. An escaped pawn was a prize to be captured and returned to its owner.

There were other fears to wrestle with as well. The low growl of a leopard rumbled faintly in Kaboo's ears. His heart fluttered in his chest. He held his breath. The sound faded into the distance. The fugitive boy relaxed. Leopards, snakes, and wild boars were among the many dangers Kaboo would have to face in the jungle.

The young boy fell into a restless sleep. His mind swirled with thoughts of the amazing thing that had happened. His father's face and his sister's soft eyes filtered through his dreams, tugging at his heart. He knew he could not go back to his own camp. It would mean certain punishment for his people. Exhaustion finally triumphed over troubling thoughts and the boy fell into a deep sleep. When he woke, he would face the jungle again.

two

As the eye of the day fanned its light through the jungle branches, Kaboo stirred and opened his eyes. For a few minutes, he lay motionless. Momentarily he forgot the horrors that had brought him to rest in a hollow tree.

Then the events crowded back: the whippings, the time in the stock, and the voice saying to him, "Flee, flee!" Finally he remembered his escape through the forest.

He crawled out of the hollow tree and fell back on the ground. With another great effort, Kaboo pulled himself upright. His throat felt dry and thirsty, and his limbs were stiff and sore.

His thirst drove him toward the sound of running water, and when he discovered a pool of fresh water, he ran to its edge, plunged his face into the water, and drank deeply. He let the water slowly run down his swollen throat. It brought new life to Kaboo.

He sighed, "I must find food." But for the moment, he lay at the water's edge, content to know that he was safe from the Grebos.

The Grebos! *Am I really safe? Would a warrior find me in this quiet space?* he wondered. *I must hurry as far away as possible. I must keep close watch for warriors.*

Instantly Kaboo was wide awake and alert. He plucked a lime from a nearby tree and rubbed it into his wounds. The lime juice smarted, but soon the swelling was gone.

Kaboo had fled so quickly that he didn't know in which direction to walk. He decided to follow the stream. It was easier to jump from rock to rock than to fight the fierce brush, which scratched and tore his flesh. As he passed overhanging berry bushes, he grasped a handful of berries. Once he lifted a rock and gathered a handful of grubs. He liked them better fried on hot stones, but he was in a hurry.

At first, the prince stopped throughout the day to listen for approaching warriors. As the day wore on, he grew more reckless. *I don't know where I'm going, but I'm glad for the good space between me and the Grebos*, he thought. He began to feel safer.

He walked rapidly. To leap from one flat stone to another was easy for him, and somehow he felt pulled onward. Each step brought feelings of freedom and safety.

As he almost reached a turn in the stream, he heard voices. Quickly Kaboo hid in the bushes beside the shallow stream. He peered around the corner and saw men watering their oxen. Holding his breath much of the time, he waited. *They are not Grebos, but they might take me back for a reward. I must be careful*, Kaboo reminded himself.

After the men left, Kaboo hurried past the watering hole. He watched carefully as the alligators slithered back to their favorite rocks. The farther he walked along the stream, he soon realized, the deeper it was becoming. The rocks were growing fewer and the alligators more numerous.

Here the banks were sandy, however, and he raced across the sand until he came to an overgrowth that forced him back into the stream. Sometimes Kaboo had to swim around the jungle growth, but he preferred to jump from rock to rock. He continued to spend his nights in trees and to follow the stream by day.

The stream widened into a river and Kaboo kept following it. As the water increased, Kaboo encountered more and more people. When he saw these people, Kaboo hid.

The days passed in a blur as the prince made his way through the forest. He crossed streams, forged rivers. Lush ferns grazed his arms and legs, vines reached out with grasping arms as if to take him captive. Mangrove swamps boiled over with mud that reached up to Kaboo's knees. Driver ants crossed the jungle path, a two-inch band of fluid movement, dangerous if disturbed by a bare foot or hand.

The black cobra, the puff adder, the boa hanging from the trees were each deadly enemies. The leopard, the lion, and the crocodile in the waters were all ready to strike as Kaboo fled through the jungle.

Not only did he want to create a huge distance between himself and the Grebos, but he was also concerned about cannibals. He had heard stories about tribes that ate their captives, and he did not want to meet up with such people.

As the distance between Kaboo and his enemies widened, the boy relaxed some. Lush treetops meshed to form a green ceiling over the forest. The sun filtered through the emerald green, sprinkling precious splatterings of light. Kaboo lost track of time. He wondered numbly where the rivers and streams would lead him. Would he ever come to the end of his wanderings?

After a few weeks, rather than hide from strangers, Kaboo felt safe enough to hurry past them without speaking. No one seemed to notice him. When he was hungry, Kaboo would pick wild bananas and mangoes to eat.

Vines trailed like aerial ropes from high branches and the jungle foliage was so thick in places that it shut out the sunlight. Ferns grew higher than a tall man's head; blossoms floated on the river. Kaboo caught his breath at the amazing beauty around him.

Gradually the river widened and the water slowed in its rushing. Early one morning, after what seemed like endless days, Kaboo heard a rooster crow. That could only mean one thing: civilization!

Kaboo looked to the southeast and his heart jumped. He strained forward and saw a large wooden house painted white. He had never seen such a structure. It had round pillars that seemed to reach as high as a tree. The roof was slate and surrounded by a white fence and dozens of glass windows. The whole place was unlike anything Kaboo had seen in any of the villages he was familiar with.

He hurried forward, then hesitated. Who were these people? Would they know he was an escaped pawn? Would they send him back to the place of horror he had left behind? Kaboo shook his head. Whoever or whatever had set him free had surely brought him this far. He had nothing to lose.

Thirsty for the sight of another human being, Kaboo crept toward the noises. A soft breeze carried a sound to the boy's ears, a sound he felt he had not heard for a lifetime. Music! Someone was singing! Crouching down, the young prince pulled aside the ferns that obscured his sight.

Before his eyes stretched a field of coffee plants. The white flowers and red berries of the plants painted the scene with bright color. After his eyes recovered from the shocking picture, he noticed that the hillsides were covered with rows of bushes and that men, women, and children were picking berries.

How strange these people look with their heads covered with cloth, he thought.

Kaboo crept closer and circled the strange fields.

The people are picking little dark brown fruits, a kind that I've never seen before. No one eats them, so why do they pick and drop them in their heavy baskets? he wondered.

Kaboo set his sights on the one who was singing. Relief swept through the tired traveler. Coming toward Kaboo was a boy about his size, who was dragging a basket. Kaboo was stunned by the boy's face. He was part of the Kru people.

Kaboo emerged shyly from the bush and crept toward the boy. It seemed sensible that he should risk being seen and seek help from this boy. Kaboo was starving and nearly naked. The skin of a monkey was his only piece of clothing.

Very slowly he neared the boy. He decided to show himself. Kaboo stepped from the trees and called out words of greeting in his Kru language, "*A nuane, a nuane.*"

The boy suddenly dropped his basket and ran forward. "Prince Kaboo! What are you doing here? Is it really you?"

Never had Prince Kaboo looked less like a prince than that day he stood in his dirty loincloth, wounded, starving, and worn out with weariness and anxiety. That anxiety lifted as he recognized the face of the boy he was facing.

"Yes, it's really me, Locust! But what are you doing here?"

"I'm picking coffee beans. This is a plantation of the Conges. I work here." As though the boy was reminded through his own words, he gathered his scattered beans into his basket and continued picking.

"Ho, Prince Kaboo, walk beside me so we can talk. It is so good to speak in Nigrite again."

"What else do you speak? And who are the Conges? I have never heard of that tribe."

"They are not a tribe," Locust explained. "They were

stolen from different tribes in Africa. They were sent to America as slaves and now are returned to Liberia as free men. These people speak English and hire many tribespeople who speak various tribal languages. So in order to talk with each other, we all learned English. But what about you? Tell me about yourself."

While the boy continued picking coffee beans, Kaboo related his adventures and finished his tale by saying, "Now I'm far from the Grebos, but I don't know what to do."

Locust suggested, "Why don't you ask for work here on the plantation? My boss is a good man. He will give you a job here on the plantation. Food and clothes." He caught the fear in Kaboo's eyes. "You are safe now, brother. I'll take you to see Mr. Davis, the owner."

Prince Kaboo looked at the boy with a worried frown, "Are you sure that he won't send me back to the Grebos?"

"No, he wouldn't do that. He was a slave himself—remember I told you!"

Just then, the bell sounded and the workers put their baskets on their heads and walked to the weighing place. Kaboo stood aside, watching the tired faces of the workers and listening to their strange sounds. Finally everyone was gone except Locust, Kaboo, and Mr. Davis.

Locust approached Mr. Davis. As he pointed to Kaboo, Locust explained his situation. Mr. Davis looked sharply at Kaboo, who appeared forlorn and lonely. Walk-ing to the prince, Mr. Davis took both his hands and spoke words that Kaboo could not understand. But

Kaboo could understand the smile, the warm, firm hands, and the welcoming look in Mr. Davis's eyes.

"He's asking you if you want to work on the plantation," Locust explained.

"Yes, yes." Kaboo's eyes widened and his teeth shone as white as the clouds. "Tell him 'a bird in hand is worth a hundred flying.' I will gladly do this, for now."

Mr. Davis patted Kaboo on the head, motioned to Locust, and pointed to a frame bunkhouse. Kaboo followed Locust to the main building. He was readily accepted and given a place to sleep in the bunkhouse. Kaboo gladly pulled on his new clothes and set out to learn the ways of the coffee plantation. He felt the cycle of terror that had ruled his life had finally come to an end.

Locust took Kaboo by the hand. "Come on. Let me show you around. The bunkhouse had boards built all around the walls; it has six places for beds in the middle. Everyone has their own mat and change of clothes. Every night you take a bath, put on the clean clothes, and are set for the next day."

"You work every day?"

"No, on Saturday we can go into town and on Sunday we go to church. And speaking of church, I am no longer called Locust. I am Nathan Strong. When you become a Christian, you get a new Christian name."

"What's a Christian?" Kaboo asked.

"You will find out, Prince Kaboo. It will be the happiest day of your life. Wait and see," Nathan promised as he led his friend to the dining room.

The two young friends sat at a table where the

workers chattered in English. Kaboo nodded to the others, but he didn't say anything. He was still stunned at the turn his life had taken.

As he adjusted to his new life, Kaboo continued to wrestle with what had transpired. He marveled at the abrupt change. One day he was hanging over a cross of wood, dying. Now he was strong and busy at work, secure and safe.

Over and over he thought about the voice and the light that had saved his life and brought him to the settlement. Who was it? It must have been some kind of spirit. Kaboo had been taught about spirits since he was a young child, but most of those spirits were to be feared and appeased with sacrifices. This Spirit was different. Kaboo was hungry for answers.

Kaboo noticed there was something different about his new friend at the plantation. One day Kaboo came into the bunkhouse and found his fellow Kru kneeling on the floor. His face and hands were turned upward. He was talking to someone.

"What are you doing?" asked the curious Kaboo.

"I am praying," replied the boy readily.

"Who are you praying to?"

"Why, I'm praying to God."

"Who is your god?" Kaboo asked, his heart pounding.

The boy looked into the young prince's eyes. "He is my Father."

Kaboo nodded. He thought it over. "Then you are

talking to your father," he decided.

The praying boy invited Kaboo to church. "Come with me to the mission this Sunday," he urged the prince. "You will hear more about God."

Kaboo attended church with his friend. He understood little of what was said, but the sense of God's presence convicted his heart. His friend explained the gospel to him. Kaboo followed the lead of his friend and began to "talk to his Father." He prayed earnestly for answers to the aching questions in his heart. *Could a poor boy like me know God? Was it God who saved me from destruction?*

three

It was almost like moving to a foreign planet for Kaboo to work on the plantation. In his Kru village, everyone had considered Kaboo as the future chief. Even the enemies, the Grebos recognized Kaboo as a prince and beat him more because of his position of leadership. On the large plantation, Kaboo was just one of the workers. It felt strange.

The boss showed Kaboo how to pick the brown coffee beans quickly and how to leave the green beans undisturbed. Then the boss showed Kaboo how to pull his basket along the row of plants while he picked the coffee. Each of these tasks became Kaboo's daily work.

Nathan showed Kaboo how to harvest coffee, shell it, dry it, and then sack it. Nathan also taught the young prince the myriad of other things he needed to know to adjust to his new work, new home, and new life.

Nathan paired up with Kaboo as they worked in the fields. They faced each other on opposite sides of one row. The end of the row seemed an eternity away.

When Kaboo looked toward it, he felt despair at the size of his job.

"Don't worry about the end, just pick," Nathan counseled. Soon the noisy chatter of the other boys filled the air. "What are they saying?" Kaboo asked.

Nathan interpreted the chatter for the prince.

"You watch," Beji said. "You said I was filling my basket too slow. Mine will be filled long before yours!"

"Oh, it will, will it? We shall see!" Tunji replied.

"Yes, we shall! We shall indeed. I shall fill two baskets before you can fill one!"

As the young prince watched, the boys reached their arms out, felt for a bean, found one, and dropped it into their basket. Quickly they reached out again.

Someone in the field began to chant a rhythmic saying. Much later Beji said, "Slow as a worm, you are. I told you I'd finish first."

Immediately the pair began another contest. Kaboo was caught up in the cheerful rhythm and found that he worked faster. But he felt insulted when Nathan finished his side and came halfway back on Kaboo's side before he could complete the row.

"Never mind, friend," Nathan said. "I was slow when I started picking coffee."

"One day I'll finish first!" Kaboo promised. "See if I don't."

Nathan laughed at his friend. "You know, it is one thing to cackle and another to lay an egg." As the day passed, Kaboo improved. The middle of the day grew hot, and Kaboo was thankful when everyone stopped a

49

few minutes for water. He noticed that after the rest, Beji and Tunji were the first to return and start picking again. He wondered if he would ever be able to work as fast as that pair.

Kaboo was amazed at the chatter of English between Beji and Tunji. He wished that he could speak English.

At the end of the day, Kaboo weighed his beans. Every part of his body ached. "This is worse than a whipping," Kaboo muttered.

"You will get used to it—honest," Nathan promised.

Mr. Davis suggested that Kaboo spend an hour every day studying English. For one hour each day, Mr. Davis's wife taught the boys to speak English. Kaboo told Nathan, "I see that I will never belong here if I don't speak and understand English."

Mrs. Davis loved to teach—even though she didn't speak a word of Kaboo's Nigrite language. She didn't let that little fact stop her teaching. Through the years, Mrs. Davis had taught many people from different tribes.

All day Kaboo listened for words that he learned in his class. He also asked Nathan about other words. For him, English was like a great puzzle that needed to be solved.

When Sunday came, Nathan urged Kaboo, "Come to church. The missionaries usually speak in English first. Then the elder repeats what was said. As you learn more English, you find yourself understanding even before the elder speaks." While Nathan was speaking to the young prince, he was twisting a cloth in his hands.

Kaboo laughed at his friend. "Twisting that cloth

won't make me come to church. I want to go to church because you said that I'd learn about Christians. Now I am curious about the change in you—about your new name. I'll go."

Though many people were waiting when the wagons rolled up, Kaboo noticed many of the workers were not there.

"Where are the others?" Kaboo asked.

"Some go into town and stay Saturday night. Some sleep. You see, Mr. Davis sends the wagons, but we don't go unless we want to," Nathan explained.

Along the way to church, Kaboo admired how the green hills sloped down to the lazy river. Many hills were covered with coffee bean bushes. As they passed other plantation homes, Kaboo said, "Tell me more about the Conges. Mr. Davis looks like us, but he is—"

"I know what you mean," Nathan broke in. "They say the former slaves from America are civilized and the elite. I guess that means they don't kill, eat, or make slaves of other people," Nathan finished lamely.

Kaboo was poised to ask another question, but it was cut short. The band of people in the creaking wagons began to sing Christian songs in English. Kaboo was transported with joy. Before these songs, his only experience with music was the beating of drums or chants. "This music flows like water," he told Nathan.

When the wagon rounded the bend, Kaboo could see the church in the distance and asked, "Why does it have a high peak?"

Nathan answered, "It points to heaven."

51

Before Kaboo could ask, "What's heaven?" the workers jumped from the wagon and Kaboo started to run toward the white church.

"Wait, Kaboo, we walk slowly into the church," Nathan cautioned his friend. "See how the others go with their heads high. We walk slowly into church."

"Why?" demanded Kaboo.

"Well, I don't know. It's civilized or Christian or something. But nobody talks or asks questions when the missionary speaks."

"I'll do whatever you do, Nathan," Kaboo promised. Then suddenly Kaboo began to question his actions. As a prince, he had moved or spoken when he wanted to do so. Suddenly he wondered if that way of behaving was correct. It was a new experience for him.

He followed Nathan to the back of the room where all of the plantation workers were seated. After they were settled, family after family of the Conges entered the building. Holding their heads high, they took their places near the front of the church. Everyone stared at the men's frock coats and stovepipe hats. They watched in wonder at the women in their gathered skirts and the children with their frocks, hose, and shoes.

Kaboo opened his mouth to ask a question, but Nathan quickly put his finger over his mouth. *Questions will have to wait,* he seemed to say to his friend. While Kaboo had been gawking at the Conges, he hadn't noticed the missionaries and the elders who had entered the room and taken their places.

Suddenly organ music filled the church. Kaboo

could not believe so many tones could come from a small box. His eyes popped open, and Nathan covered his lips once more.

The Conges opened their books and, with a signal from a man in front, began singing with the organ music. Most of the plantation workers knew the songs and sang the words whether they understood them or not. Evidently there were not enough books for everyone.

With awe, Kaboo listened to the music. His soul felt soothed. The talking, however, excited him. The missionaries' words in English were not understandable, and the interpretation was in another native language. But he did understand the earnest expressions on their faces.

Prince Kaboo sat spellbound. *I must learn about this God,* he thought, and dreams of how that might happen filled his mind on the trip back to the plantation.

Every day Mrs. Davis began the English class the same way. She asked, "How many ears do you have?"

The class answered in unison, "We have two ears!"

"Then add a third, and listen to what I have to tell you!"

She never explained what she meant about the third ear, but Kaboo listened to her teaching. First, he understood "ears," then "two ears," then "listen." Finally the meaning filled his head. He grinned and nodded, "Yes, Mrs. Davis, I will listen with three ears, here and everywhere!" He whispered these words under his breath. It had taken awhile, but Kaboo had finally learned not to speak out loud.

The prince learned English everywhere, not only in the classroom but at every opportunity. When he went to town with Nathan, he discovered more new words. Learning and understanding was one thing, but writing and speaking those words was something completely different.

As Kaboo entered the bunkhouse one day, he saw Nathan on his knees with both of his hands lifted up and his face turned toward the roof. "What are you doing?" Kaboo asked.

"I'm talking to God."

"Who is your God: the god of the Kru people or the God in the church?"

Nathan answered, "In a way, they are all the same, the Creator. Remember we learned God created man so that the sun would have someone for whom to shine? Then God created plants and animals for food for man; then a wife so man would have someone to talk with."

"Is this what the missionaries teach?" Kaboo asked with some doubts.

"Almost the same," Nathan nodded.

"Well, what is different?" Kaboo pressed his friend.

Nathan took a deep breath. "Well, you know how we had a god of war, a god of sickness, a god of the lake, a god of cattle, and all those other gods?"

"Yes."

"The missionaries tell us that there is only one God. He is all powerful, all strong, all knowing," Nathan explained.

"And what about the spirits and the living dead?"

"The Christians believe in one Spirit, the Holy Ghost."

"And the living dead?"

"When a person dies, Christians believe his soul goes to heaven if he was a believer—and to hell if he was not."

Kaboo asked, "Then he doesn't stay and watch his people? There is no need to make altars and leave food for the living dead?"

"No, not at all."

Kaboo's eyes filled with tears as he heard his friend's words. "I found this was true during the night of the Grebos' attack. I thought I was the only one who knew that the living dead were not there. Poor Margol!"

The two friends continued talking for a long time. Kaboo finally asked, "And who is your God, Nathan?"

"He is my Father."

"Then you hold up your hands, kneel, and talk to your Father. Let's do it now." Kaboo knelt with Nathan.

The next Sunday, Kaboo knelt again, but this time he was in the churchyard. A new missionary had arrived, Miss Anna Knolls from Fort Wayne, Indiana. She said, "The story I am going to tell you is found in the Bible in the Book of Acts." The interpreter faithfully translated to the audience whatever the missionary spoke.

"It is a story about a man named Saul. He was filled with hatred for Jesus and His followers. He wanted all the believers in Jesus to be captured and put in prison."

Kaboo listened intently.

55

"One day this man was on the road traveling to a certain town in order to arrest all the followers of Christ. He was going to drag them away from their homes and imprison them."

Kaboo flinched. He knew what it was like to be taken from his home and held captive. He sat forward in his seat.

"While Saul traveled on the road, a strange thing happened. A bright light from heaven burst upon him. He fell to the ground, blind. Then he heard a voice speaking."

Miss Knolls paused, her eyes sparkling. "It was Jesus! Saul's life was changed forever! He became a Christian! Saul became a champion of the very gospel he had tried to destroy. The light of the gospel had come to him and saved him from a hate-filled and destructive way of life."

As the interpreter relayed to the listeners what Miss Knolls said about Saul, Kaboo's face lit up. He leapt up from his seat.

"That light! That voice! It happened to me!" he cried. "When they were whipping me and I was about to die, I heard that voice. I saw that light!" His face glowed with the revelation. "Now I know who it was who saved my life. It was Jesus!"

The gathering of people stared at the boy, astonished. Miss Knolls signaled to the interpreter to close the meeting. She headed for the young boy, and with the help of the interpreter, Kaboo told her his story. His testimony took her breath away.

"So now I know whose voice it was that told me to run," beamed the boy. "It was the voice of Jesus. What He did for that man Saul, He did for me."

Miss Knolls nodded. "Would you like to know more about Jesus?" she asked.

"Oh yes," Kaboo replied eagerly. "Tell me everything."

Miss Knolls let out a joyful laugh. "You are a missionary's dream come true!" she said.

Miss Knolls took Kaboo aside and sat him down on a bench. She explained to Kaboo the story of Jesus' life and his mission on earth.

Kaboo could readily understand the concept of Jesus being taken as a pawn to save the lives of sinners. Tears streamed down his ebony face as Miss Knolls told how the Father gave up His Son as a pawn and how the blood of Jesus was the payment made to redeem the people of the world. Sons and daughters were reconciled with their Father in heaven because the price was paid.

"I believe in this Jesus," said Kaboo softly. "His Father is my Father now."

Miss Knolls looked with joy at the African boy. God had done a mighty work. He had brought the boy out of darkness into the light. She was thrilled that she could play a small part in Kaboo's story. A new missionary to Africa, Miss Knolls did not come from a wealthy family. Reared in Fort Wayne, Indiana, she had been educated in the public schools and at Taylor University, formerly named Methodist Episcopal College. Seen as a promising student, Miss Knolls came to the attention of a well-to-do banker and philanthropist who paid most of her college expenses and inspired her to missionary service.

Miss Knolls took Kaboo under her wing, teaching him some English. He hungrily listened to the Bible stories and lessons she taught him. Kaboo was thirsty to know more about God. Little by little, Kaboo learned the beautiful story of Jesus' birth in a manger; His ministry to the humble, the sinful, and the diseased; His atoning death and resurrection. Kaboo readily accepted this newfound Savior of souls as the same "unknown God" who had saved his body when death had seemed so certain.

But Kaboo was not satisfied. Like almost every new Christian, he soon became conscious that his redemption from the guilt and penalty of past sins did not free him from continued failings in his daily actions. His body continued to bear the scars from his many beatings as a pawn of the Grebos. His mind had grown accustomed to fear and hate during his years of cruel suffering. His beatings among the Grebos made him feel hopelessly inferior. He could see no future for himself apart from a miracle.

Unknown to Kaboo, God has provided such a miracle for every believer through the work of the Holy Ghost. Slowly Kaboo understood his new life in Christ. He began to understand that his new life in Christ and in the Spirit purified his heart of all bitterness. It enabled the Christian to serve God.

Kaboo was happy. "Like the boy Samuel in the Bible, God spoke to me," he said to Miss Knolls. "How lucky I am!"

"Lucky? Kaboo, we're not talking about luck," Miss Knolls said. "Can't you see that God has chosen you?"

Kaboo took his teacher's words to heart. Prayer became the focus of the young prince's life. He talked to his Father constantly. Despite his understanding of the gospel, a restlessness stirred in Kaboo's heart. He felt deeply the need to serve God. He longed to be able to preach to his own Kru people in their own language the same good news of God's love that had brought such peace to his own soul.

But Kaboo felt his utter lack of fitness and authority for such a mission in life. He felt inadequate and unworthy. Years of abuse and suffering had shattered his sense of worth. A childhood spent in fear and bondage had broken his spirit.

How can I serve such a one as the living God? Kaboo wondered.

Day and night he struggled in prayer. He agonized in prayer, crying out to God. His earnest cries were getting on his bunkmates' nerves. They told him if he was going to pray at night, he would have to pray in the jungle.

Kaboo's new house of prayer became the forest. Among the trees and vines, he lifted up his heart to his Father. Monkeys chattered back to him. Brilliantly colored birds threaded swiftly through the trees in flashes of blues, reds, and yellows. At night, the moon laced the trees in silver. Kaboo cried out to his Father. He needed Him so! He needed to give himself completely over to the Lord. The boy was desperate for God.

One night he prayed earnestly until midnight. He returned to the bunkhouse, exhausted. He flopped down on his bunk. Worn out, he lay quietly. Though his lips were silent, his heart kept right on praying. Suddenly, the room began to brim with light. Kaboo turned over, thinking for a moment that the sun was rising. But his bunkmates continued to sleep deeply. They did not stir as they usually did when the sun rose. No rooster was crowing. It was not the morning sun.

Kaboo sat up. The room was flooded with glorious light and with glory. At that moment, the heavy weight on Kaboo's heart was taken away. The burden was replaced with joy such as he had never experienced. He felt light as a feather.

"Praise God!" Kaboo shouted, jumping up from his bunk. "Praise God!" He continued to shout and leap for joy. "I am His son! He is my Father!"

His roommates woke up to the glorious commotion. They stared at the Kru boy from the interior.

"What's going on?" someone mumbled sleepily.

"It's Kaboo," came a reply. "I think he's gone crazy!"

Another man sat up, wide-eyed. "It must be a demon has got him," he said fearfully.

Kaboo could only laugh and shout for joy. His burden was gone. He knew he was in the arms of a Father who would never disappear in the jungle or be unable to care for him. He knew the One who had touched his arm at the horrible wooden cross and set him free now held him with everlasting arms. Kaboo had become His son.

The next day, Kaboo hurried to tell Miss Knolls what had happened. The missionary listened in amazement.

"It was my adoption, Miss Knolls," said Kaboo joyfully. "God has made me His own son."

The missionary choked back tears. How could this boy, unschooled in the Scriptures, possibly know about the theological concept of adoption?

Another miracle, thought Miss Knolls. *Surely the hand of God is on this boy's life.*

She pulled out her Bible and read aloud Romans 8:15: "For you have not received the spirit of bondage again to fear; but you have received the Spirit of adoption, whereby we cry Abba, Father."

Kaboo vigorously nodded his head. "Yes, that's it! God came to me last night. He has adopted Kaboo!"

four

K aboo's experience with the Lord changed him. He was a different person, filled with joy and confidence in his Father. The Lord had saved him, healed him from his painful past, and filled him with the Holy Ghost. He was hungry for the Lord. As often as he could, he spent time with the missionaries to learn more from them.

Miss Knolls taught Kaboo about water baptism. He readily agreed to be baptized in the name of the Lord. When Kaboo came out of the water, Miss Knolls stood up to speak.

"My parents were poor," she said, her voice trembling. "But it was my heart's desire to serve the Lord as a missionary. I needed training. But how could I go to school with no money?" She paused and smiled at Kaboo.

"The Lord has a way of providing when we cannot provide for ourselves. A banker named Samuel Morris heard about my plight and generously paid for my education at Taylor University. I stand here today with Kaboo, the first African boy I have seen come to Christ. And so in keeping with our custom of giving new believers American names, I would like to give Kaboo the name of the one who made it possible for me to be here, Samuel Morris."

Miss Knolls turned to face Kaboo. "From now on, you will be called Samuel Morris," she told him, beaming.

Kaboo smiled. "It is a good name," he said. "Like the Samuel in the Bible, right?"

Miss Knolls nodded and shook his hand. "Congratulations on your baptism, Samuel."

"Thank you," responded the new believer.

Sammy (as he soon was called by all who knew him) was an avid student. When he wasn't working hard in the coffee fields, he was learning Bible stories from Miss Knolls. She also tutored him in the English language. He spent two years at the plantation. Then Miss Knolls suggested that Sammy move to Monrovia, where the mission had its headquarters. She cautioned him to spend his money wisely and introduced him to a house painter.

"Come be my helper," said the painter. "The Conges have built a great college here, and I am commissioned to paint it. You can sleep on a mat in the rooms we are painting and take your meals with the missionaries."

"And what about Nathan?" Sammy asked.

"Nathan can come, too. I have also hired a third boy, Alabo. You three will have much work to do."

Sammy and Nathan decided to work for this painter.

In spite of Miss Knoll's warning, Sammy soon spent his money. He bought clothes, a mat, and a pair of strange scissors. He cut his own hair and Nathan's. His system was simple. He cut off almost all his hair. Soon he had a curly cap that was quite comfortable.

"Alabo, let me cut your hair, too," Sammy offered as the boys lay on their mats after working all day.

"How did you learn to cut hair?" Alabo asked.

"Look this way. See how I cut mine. Look at Nathan; I cut his hair, too," Sammy encouraged.

"Oh, all right," Alabo agreed, "but be careful with the points of those scissors. I don't want to lose an eye."

Sammy loved his new life in the city. He liked his work, his new friends, and the close contact with the missionaries. When they ran out of paint, Sammy would hunt for the missionaries. There were several near Monrovia besides Miss Knolls. The Reverend C. E. Smirl and Miss MacNeil spent hours answering Sammy's questions. For two years, Sammy learned nearly everything that he could.

He passed his knowledge on to Nathan and took Alabo under his wing as well. Sammy invited Alabo to church and introduced him to the missionaries. Then he talked with Alabo about God.

"What does your tribe say of the first man and woman?"

Alabo found that to be an easy question. "Ho, we learn they had everything they wanted in paradise."

"What happened?"

"God told them not to eat the eggs of the birds," Nathan responded.

"Did they eat them?" Sammy questioned further.

"Yes, they ate and God separated from them."

"Was there a way to get back to God?" Sammy persisted.

"No, no way."

"That is how Christianity is different," Sammy said. "The Bible shows a way to God. He sent His Son, Jesus Christ, to take the punishment of man. Jesus made a way by dying in place of all men—for all sin."

For a time, Alabo sat in silence. Then he asked, "What do I have to do to get God?"

" 'Believe on the Lord Jesus Christ, and thou shalt be saved,' " Sammy answered. He was glad that he had memorized this verse from the Bible and could recite it to Alabo.

"That's all you have to do—just believe in Jesus?" Alabo asked in an incredible tone.

"That's all that He asks!" Sammy paused, then knelt, raised his hands to heaven, and prayed.

Alabo soon followed the example of his friend. "O God, I believe in your Son, Jesus Christ. Save my soul." Sammy's heart was filled with joy at his friend's decision.

With every spare moment, Sammy helped the missionaries. One afternoon with fear and trembling, Sammy gave his first testimony. Miss Knolls helped him with the English words. "Ask the Holy Ghost to help you to be brave," she suggested.

Once Sammy began speaking, his fear left him and he could tell his audience, "God spoke to me. He said, 'Flee, Flee'; so I ran away from the Grebos. God directed me to the plantation. I could have been eaten by cannibals or harmed by wild beasts, but God protected me. He led

65

Miss Knolls around the world to tell me about Jesus, my Savior. I thank Him." Sammy sat down and sighed with exhaustion from talking about Jesus in another language.

Sammy was eager to learn from all of the missionaries. He especially loved to hear their songs of praise to God. He learned many of the hymns by heart. It was obvious to the believers who came in contact with Sammy that the presence of the Lord was with this dedicated young man. When he prayed, things happened!

One American missionary worker among the Kru people was named Nancy Minor. She and two native women were anxious to see the whole community accept Jesus Christ as its Savior. To carry out this goal, they agreed to conduct prayer meetings starting at midnight and lasting until daylight. These continued for several months and increased their desire to see the people of Monrovia come to Christ.

One dark, still night, the three women were joined by a native boy who silently entered the meeting and prostrated himself near the pulpit, where he prayed for hours. They assumed he had come to accept Christ as his Savior.

Leaving the boy undisturbed in his prayers, the women went from door to door and told the good news to other church members. When they returned, they learned that this boy was none other than Samuel Morris. He had come, not to find Jesus Christ for himself, but to pray that others might know the heavenly Father. For hours Sammy pleaded for the souls of the people.

At the evangelistic meetings that followed, fifty people

accepted Christ as their Savior and Lord. The three women rejoiced and praised God for sending Sammy to their prayer meeting.

One day to Sammy's surprise, he met a young Kru boy whom he recognized. It was a boy from his own village! The boy had been captured by the same Grebo chief and kept as a slave. He was there when Sammy had been tortured.

"Kaboo!" cried the astonished boy. "You are alive! I can't believe it!"

Sammy nodded. The memory of his miraculous escape flashed through his mind. "It is a miracle I can stand here and talk with you!"

"Tell me what happened!" said the boy excitedly. "You know I was there when they tortured you. I knew you were dying—the beatings were getting so bad. But then that one night—"

Sammy grabbed the boy's arm. "You mean you saw—"

"I saw everything!" yelped the boy, his hands gesturing fervently. "I remember how the strange light suddenly flashed over you. I heard someone call to you!" The boy's eyes widened at the thought of it. "And then, suddenly," he whispered, "you were gone! What happened, Kaboo? What happened to you?"

The young prince's eyes filled with tears of joy. His heart thrilled because he could indeed explain those miraculous events to his fellow Kru and introduce him to Jesus.

"It was the Lord, my friend!" exclaimed Sammy. "The

67

light you saw and the voice you heard belonged to Jesus. He saved my life!" Kaboo placed his hands on the astonished boy's shoulders. "He not only saved my life, but He has also saved my soul. He has made me His own. God is now my Father! I will never be alone again!"

The other boy's eyes filled with longing. Such comforting words! Such wondrous hope the prince was holding out to him. Sammy searched his friend's face and read the desire written there.

"He can be your Father, too," spoke the prince softly. "Would you like to pray with me?"

The boy nodded. Together they knelt and Sammy introduced his friend to Jesus.

Sammy presented the new Christian to his missionary friends. They promptly baptized him, giving him the name Henry O'Neill. Together, Sammy and Henry shared the testimony of their salvation. Many listened with wonder as Sammy talked of his miraculous escape. Henry's eyewitness account of the miracle added to the power of their testimony.

After meeting his friend Henry, Sammy's heart was filled with an even more urgent desire to go back to his own people and share the gospel with them. He was burdened about the people around him who had not yet turned to Jesus. They were a desolate picture of sin and bondage. His burden became an intense weight that was difficult to ignore.

He traveled many miles to speak about his concern with the Reverend C. E. Smirl. Pastor Smirl was the man who headed up the missionary work in Monrovia.

"Reverend Smirl, what must I do to be a missionary?" Sammy asked.

"You cannot just go back to your tribe, even if it were safe. You are not ready. You are lacking in education," Mr. Smirl said as he held up a heavy book. "If you want to be a preacher, you must get an education."

"An education?" asked Sammy. "And where should I go to get an education?"

"You can go to America. It only costs a hundred dollars for a fare across the ocean," Mr. Smirl encouraged. "Save your money. Work long hours like Nathan."

One hundred dollars was a huge sum of money to Sammy. He didn't have that kind of money. But instead of worrying about it, that night Sammy went to the forest and prayed for many hours to his Father. "Father," he cried out, "the missionary told me that I must be educated, and to be educated I must go to America. How can I, for I do not have the hundred dollars to pay?"

Leaving the woods just before daylight, Sammy was confident that the Lord would prepare a way. Prayer with his heavenly Father calmed his heart. Day after day, he lay in wait for a ship that would take him to America.

Meanwhile, Sammy also felt a great desire to learn more about the land where he was going—America. One day Sammy prayed and decided to visit another missionary, Lizzie MacNeil. She lived at a mission located several miles from Monrovia. The long walk left him with throbbing feet, but when he entered the last dusty path to the mission outpost, he forgot about his feet.

"Ho, Miss MacNeil!" he called.

"Who comes to my door? Oh, Sammy, welcome. I'm so glad that you came—just in time for devotions." Wearing a baggy sweater, flowing skirt, and bedroom slippers, Miss MacNeil held the screen door open.

Sammy stepped inside the shack. Clutter was everywhere. Books and papers were open where Miss MacNeil had stopped reading. Her broken sofa served as her bed and was covered with crumpled blankets and pillows. Hurriedly Miss MacNeil rolled up these blankets and tucked them away.

Sammy liked Miss MacNeil. *She cannot be bothered with the things of this world because she is so full of the Bible,* he thought.

Miss MacNeil spoke freely of a subject that was unfamiliar to Sammy—the Holy Ghost. Others had diligently taught him the truths of the gospel of Jesus Christ. No one had ever spoken of the Holy Ghost like Miss MacNeil. Sammy was captivated. To be sure, he had already experienced the infilling of the Holy Ghost, but he did not know that he could become acquainted with the Holy Ghost.

Miss MacNeil shared her testimony with her eager student. "When I was ready to go overseas to serve the Lord as a missionary, I was excited and frightened at the same time. I was a young girl from the far west of the United States. I traveled to New York to be sent out by Bishop Taylor. I was met by Stephen Merritt, Bishop Taylor's secretary. He could see that I was feeling a bit overwhelmed."

The woman's voice softened at the memory. "The

secretary began to speak to me about the Holy Ghost. He told me if I would humble myself before the Lord and wholly commit myself to Him, I would be filled with the Holy Ghost. The Holy Ghost would empower me to be a vital witness of the gospel in Africa. His words stirred a yearning in my heart.

"We prayed together, and I was filled to overflowing with the Holy Ghost of God. When it came time to board the ship that would bear me to Africa, I was ready to go! The Comforter was with me in a way I had never experienced before."

She laughed. "My companions thought I would not do well in Africa! They would watch me as I sat alone on the boat. As I communed with the Lord in prayer, I would sometimes laugh, sometimes cry, at times just talk quietly with Him. My friends thought I was heartbroken over leaving behind a lost lover!" Miss MacNeil laughed again. "Little did they know, I had come aboard with my greatest love—the Lord!"

Sammy's heart leaped for joy at her words. His talks with his Father were as sweet and intimate as the times of prayer this missionary friend was telling him about.

"Please teach me more about the Holy Ghost," implored Sammy. "I want to know more about Him." So Miss MacNeil opened her Bible for the young African. She highlighted the truths in the Word concerning the Holy Ghost.

"The Scriptures teach us that the Holy Ghost is not a ghostly force. He is a counselor, a comforter. We can know Him, and we are instructed to be led by Him, to keep in step with Him."

She smiled at the eagerness in her student. "Listen to what it says in the fourteenth chapter of John's Gospel: 'If you love me, keep my commandments. And I will pray the Father, and He shall give you another Comforter, that He may stay with you forever. Even the Spirit of truth, whom the world cannot receive, because it sees Him not, neither knows Him. But you know Him, for He dwells with you and shall be in you. I will not leave you orphans, I will come to you.' "

Sammy's eyes filled with tears of joy. "It is so true!" he cried. "I surely felt like an orphan boy before the Lord came and made me His own. Tell me more!"

When Sammy first understood that the Spirit of God worked on earth and was an actual, living Person, he had no words adequate to express his wonderment and happiness. He found it easy to attribute the mysterious voice that had led to his escape from the Grebos to God's Spirit. The Spirit had spoken to him, as to Samuel of old, before he knew it was the Lord.

In the days that followed, Sammy made repeated trips to visit Miss MacNeil and talk about the Holy Ghost. The fourteenth chapter of John became Sammy's constant study. Miss MacNeil continued to explain about the work of the Holy Ghost. She taught Sammy that it was the Holy Ghost who opens the Word to the be-liever, who reveals Jesus to us, who empowers us to live for Christ.

Sammy asked countless questions. He spent hours

72

listening and learning. His hunger for God was strong. He wanted to know the Lord, wanted to walk with Him and glorify His name.

Finally, the missionary could teach her student no more.

"Sammy, I've taught you all I know. I wish I could tell you more, but I can't!" She smiled at the young prince. "I've given you all I've got. As it is, I've repeated most of it many times over!"

Sammy's face wrinkled with consternation. "Well then," he said simply, "who taught you about the Holy Ghost?"

"Stephen Merritt. He was the secretary to Bishop Taylor whom I told you about. He taught me everything I know about the Holy Ghost."

"Where is Stephen Merritt?" pressed the earnest young man.

"In America, in a city called New York," came the reply.

"I will go to see him!" Sammy said at once. Without another word, Sammy bade his teacher good-bye.

"Where are you going, Sammy?" she asked curiously.

The young man turned, his head tilted quizzically, as if he marveled that she didn't know where he was going.

"Why, I'm going to America to see Stephen Merritt. He will teach me more about the Holy Ghost." Sammy smiled and nodded farewell.

The amazed woman watched him go. Her own heart stirred at the sight of a young man whose only passion was to know the Lord—a young man who would go wherever he had to in order to learn more about Him.

When Sammy arrived back in Monrovia, he told Miss Knolls of his decision to go to New York. She objected, saying, "But Sammy, what of your job; what of helping the missionaries; what of your singing and your English lessons?"

Sammy had only one answer, "We have a saying: 'You cannot hold on to two cows' tails at the same time.'"

five

"O Father, help me," Sammy prayed. "Let there be a ship in the harbor." He was walking to the seashore. "O, God, help me get to New York. Please help me."

In time Sammy smelled the salt water and felt the warm moist breeze touch his cheeks. "It is not much farther," he told himself. Peace flooded his heart, as though God had quieted his heart with an answer to his prayers.

Sammy's first glimpse of the seaport showed him a ship anchored in the bay. "Thank you, Father," he said. The water pulsated with shimmering light. Shielding his eyes from the bright afternoon sun, Sammy talked to his Father.

The ship was known as a tramp ship. Usually these ships were owned by their captain and stopped at almost every port along the coast to buy and sell merchandise. This type of business held a great advantage for the trader. The native people usually gave their products to the traders for such worthless pay as rum, trinkets, and bright cheap cloth.

After Sammy prayed, he knew the ship was the one that would carry him to America. He dug his bare feet into the warm sand and waited patiently for someone from the ship to come by. While he was watching, a sailor passed by and Sammy asked, "Where is the ship headed?"

"New York, North America," the sailor replied.

As Sammy drew closer, a small boat pulled off the ship and headed to shore. All of the men were white. That didn't bother Sammy. The missionaries he knew were white, and they had been very kind.

He watched as the men stepped ashore, and he noticed a man giving orders in English. *That must be the captain!* he decided. He waited until the captain was near and then cried out, "Excuse me, sir. My Father told me you would take me to America in your ship to see Stephen Merritt."

Startled, the captain asked, "And where is your father?"

"He is in heaven," replied Sammy as he looked the captain directly in the eye.

The captain swore the first oath that Sammy had heard in English. Then the captain looked at his companions. He rolled his eyes and snorted with disgust. "I don't take passengers. Especially black passengers," he spat. "You must be crazy! Out of my way or I'll kick you!" He strode past Sammy, shoving him aside.

Sammy watched the captain and his men walk away. He was not discouraged by the captain's refusal. He knew what his Father had said. "The captain must come back here to get into his small boat," Sammy reasoned.

76

"I will not move from this spot." Sammy sat down next to the boat and waited. All day Sammy waited. He had nothing to eat but dared not leave.

Late that night the crew returned. To the captain's chagrin, the African boy was still on the beach, standing next to the boat. The boy approached the captain again. "Please, Mr. Captain, take me to New York! Please!"

The captain kicked in Sammy's direction. "I'll give you a swift kick if you don't stop bothering me. I will not take you!" The captain boarded his boat and set off with several drunk sailors.

"Oh, yes, you will!" Sammy shouted.

Sammy lay down on the sand. He spent the night praying on the seashore. "Father, please change the captain's mind." He felt assured that the next time he talked to the captain, he would receive a favorable answer. Sammy fell asleep with a smile on his face.

Although Sammy had had nothing to eat for two days, he stayed on the spot. The next morning the captain and a few crewmen again came ashore. All day they hauled the cargo they had acquired to the ship. Sammy helped out in any way he could. When finally he saw the captain, he spoke to him with quiet confidence. "My Father says you will let me come with you this time," he said with a smile.

The captain was tempted to give the young man a swift kick. But two of his crew had deserted the ship the night before. Now he was shorthanded. He would need this boy to work. The man rubbed the steely stubble on his chin.

"You are a Kru, right?" the captain said, having known experienced Kru sailors in the past. "What do you want for pay?"

"Just take me to New York to see Stephen Merritt," Sammy replied. "That's all I ask."

"All right," said the captain. "You can join my crew." He set his steely eyes on the boy. *He's a strange one,* he thought. He signaled to his men to let the boy get in to the boat. Little did the captain know that Sammy was not an experienced sailor.

Sammy's face glowed with joy as the oars of the boat cut into the water, propelling them toward the ship. His Father's promise was coming to pass. Sammy was on his way to America. He was on his way to gaining his heart's desire—more knowledge about the Holy Ghost of God. Sammy was about to leave his homeland of Africa.

Not a soul on the shore wished him good-bye or Godspeed. His mother was not there to give him a tearful kiss of farewell; his father was not there to speak words of counsel. Gradually as the boat ploughed through the water, Sammy saw his native land slowly fade in the distance. The three masts of the three-hundred-fifty-foot ship pointed toward the azure sky. Sammy climbed aboard and waited for the captain's orders.

Lying on the deck, Sammy found a young man with a wound in his leg. Sammy knelt down and prayed for him, then asked for water and bandages to bind up the fellow's leg.

When the grateful youth regained his strength, he

said, "I'm Harold, the cabin boy. Who are you?" He heard Sammy's story and realized the Kru had not eaten for several days.

"Leaping lizards, you must be hungry!" Harold said to Sammy as he led him to the galley.

The cook, however, refused. "I ain't got no orders to feed him," he stated. And he called Sammy a name.

Harold hid Sammy from the cook. Then he requested food for himself and shared with Sammy.

"What did the cook mean?" Sammy asked.

Harold looked blankly at Sammy. "Oh, lots of people call others names because of their color. I think they are fools, but there is one such person onboard, a Malay. You better stay out of *his* way."

"Just because I'm black?" Sammy asked. "All of my Kru people are black. The only gray or white people that I've seen until now are the missionaries, and they were good."

Harold looked at his new friend with pity, then said, "The sailors on this ship are as bad as the missionaries were good. Watch yourself."

The captain ordered his men to weigh anchor. The ship pulled away from the harbor. Liberia disappeared into the distance.

"This is my boat," boomed the captain. "She's a tramp vessel, only three-hundred-fifty feet long. It makes for a rough ride." He peered at the Kru boy who stood before him. "You're an experienced boatman, I assume? You are a Kru. How long have you worked on the coast? What's your specialty?"

Sammy shook his head. "I have no experience on boats. My people did not live on the coast."

The captain's mouth spewed forth curses. "You mean you lived in the interior? You're not from the coast? You're worthless to me!" He started for the young man. "I ought to throw you overboard right now and save myself a heap of trouble." He glowered at Kaboo. "You haven't been sick until you've been seasick! You won't be able to do any work!"

"Please, sir, do not be angry," pleaded Kaboo. "I will work for you every day until we reach New York. I will be able to work, you'll see."

Harold stepped up. "Please take him, Captain. He helped me. He is strong and willing. Also he prayed for me, and I was suddenly healed. Please keep this boy."

"I must be crazy," the captain admitted looking at the pair. "I know better, but something tells me to keep him. You'll work the masts. Clancey!" he yelled to one of his men. "Show this idiot how to reef the sails. I want him working the mast."

"I won't disappoint you, sir," responded Sammy. "I will work hard. I must get to New York to see Stephen Merritt."

The captain walked away shaking his head. *That boy just doesn't give up,* he thought.

After that, every word that was said to Sammy was accompanied by a kick or a slap. Curses and vile language rained on his head. It was just as well he didn't understand all the words. Life onboard the ship was a continuous round of cruelty.

The captain was a hard bargainer and a harsh master. He did a great deal of business with the Middle Eastern traders when they came to the coast. It was a case of an eye for an eye and a tooth for a tooth. The captain had been hardened by several such ruthless encounters. Life or death was at his command onboard his ship.

All the crew lived in dread of the captain. It was a motley group picked up from different countries around the world. Sammy was the only black and was resented at once. The men impatiently taught him to work the mast, cursing and cuffing him at every turn. But Sammy was filled with the Holy Ghost. His peace was boundless. He bore each indignity with patience and forgiveness. A supernatural strength and kindness flowed through him. Although Sammy did not like climbing up the mast, he worked diligently at his task.

Securing the sails was hard work; in windy conditions it was especially difficult. Three days back out to sea, a tropical storm burst forth with fury. Sammy was tied to his mast so he could reef the sails without falling overboard. The darkened sky brooded over the tramp vessel with vengeance. Strong winds tore at the boat, causing it to turn on its side again and again. The winds roared and the ocean answered with boiling foam and roiling waves.

Sammy told the Lord he was not afraid of the storm. "I know You will take care of me. But Father, I do not like being up on the mast. Please make a way for me to do a different job."

Each time the boat groaned to its side, Sammy was

immersed in the sea. He gagged on the salty water, swallowing large amounts. It made him violently ill. His arms fell weakly to his sides. He was helpless.

The worse part was the spray that stung the boy's flesh, blinded his eyes, and chilled him to the bone. At last the sailors untied him and brought him down to the foot of the mast, Sammy fell in a heap. The captain walked by and kicked Sammy. "I knew you'd get sick and be of no use!" He walked away without giving further thought to the stricken young man.

Sammy immediately began to speak to the One who knew him best and loved him most. While the deck pitched and heaved and water swept by Sammy, the sick young man lifted up his hands and his heart to his Father.

"Father, you know I made a promise to the captain to work for him every day until we reach New York. I cannot work when I am so sick. Please take this sickness from me, Father."

The Lord answered His child's prayer, and the sailors gasped when Sammy got up from the deck, restored to health. He was never sick again aboard the ship. The next afternoon, Harold came up to him, saying, "Sam, I heard you praying during that storm. I don't like it below decks, and you are not trained to work in the rigging. Let's trade places."

"Thank You, Lord, for answering my prayer," Sammy murmured.

"The only thing I hate is that I won't see much of you anymore," he told Harold.

Harold clasped Sammy's hand and said, "We always know we are friends."

Promptly Sammy reported to the captain for duty. As he walked toward the captain's quarters, he whispered a heartfelt thanks to his Father. The door to the cabin was ajar. As Sammy entered the room, the captain looked up from his desk in a drunken stupor. His eyes focused on the ebony figure that stood before him.

"What are you doing here?" he demanded, his voice thick with liquor.

Sammy explained the trade he had made with the cabin boy. Without a word, the cruel captain raised his fist and knocked the young man unconscious to the filthy floor. Sammy lay on the floor for several hours. When he regained consciousness, he began working around the cabin as cheerfully as if nothing had happened. He picked up his rags and bucket of water and began to clean the cabin. Somewhat sobered, the captain watched the boy in amazement.

Not only did Sammy not retaliate, but there was a look of peace on his face. As Sammy worked, he sang about Jesus. The captain's mind flooded with memories of his mother. "She sang the same songs to me when I was a boy," the captain marveled. "She taught me, 'What is learned in the cradle lasts till the grave.'" The power of forgiveness touched the rough man's heart.

Sammy looked over at the captain. "Do you know about Jesus?" he asked.

At the name of Jesus, faint recollections of Sunday

school and Bible verses floated to the surface of the captain's heart.

"May I pray for you?" asked Sammy.

The captain nodded. He listened as Sammy prayed that the captain would discover the love of God in Jesus Christ. Something began to stir in the captain's heart. He yearned for the peace and strength that the young Kru possessed. After prayer, he left Sammy and went to inspect the ship for damage from the storm. The captain's stubbled face was wrinkled in thought. There was something about Samuel Morris that he just couldn't understand.

Because the storm wrenched the superstructure of the ship, the captain anchored to the leeward of a small, uncharted island. While the caulkers and carpenters were busy, the rest of the crew manned the pumps. Pumps were utilized to keep water from capsizing the boat. Sammy was assigned to one of the many pumps. He was expected to keep up with the seasoned sailors. He pumped and prayed and prayed and pumped.

In an attempt to keep the crew in good spirits while doing such arduous work, the captain supplied the men with rum and cane juice. The alcohol burned in the men's veins. They became loose with their tongues. Tempers flared. Sammy became the butt of cruel jibes and threats.

"There, Sammy, have some rum. 'Twill warm yer insides," one of the sailors invited.

"No, no," Sam refused. "The Holy Ghost will warm me and give me strength." Sammy said it bravely, but when the pains of fatigue almost overpowered him, he began to pray again. For two weeks, they pumped. Sammy was about to faint when they hoisted the anchor and moved. While Sammy didn't realize it at the time, his hard work at the pumps had earned most of the sailors' respect.

One man in particular hated Sammy. He was the Malayan that Sammy's friend Harold had warned him about. Cruel and cold-hearted, the Malayan carried a large knife at all times. He wasn't afraid to use it on any man who came against him. The man despised Africans and often boasted that he would kill the Kru boy whenever he got the chance.

His chance came. The captain ordered extra rations of rum to celebrate the lifting of the anchor. The drinking resulted in the usual commotion of hard laughter and hard talk. As the sun dipped low, a free-for-all fight broke out among the men. The Malayan took offense. He pulled out his cutlass, his eyes glittering darkly with hatred. He would cut to pieces the ones who had taunted him.

Suddenly a small dark form stood in the Malayan's path. It was Sammy.

"Don't kill, don't kill," Sammy pleaded, his hand upraised.

"Don't kill!" laughed the Malayan, seeing his chance to kill Sammy. "I've killed many a black, you can believe. I hate blacks, I do! Get out of my way, or I'll kill you—now!"

He lifted his cutlass above his head and murder sparked in his eyes.

Sammy stood his ground and looked at the man straight in the eye. The compassion burning on Sammy's face met and overcame the hatred in the Malayan's eyes. The angry man shivered because of God's power. He lowered his weapon, turned, and walked away.

The sailors watching the scene had fully expected to see blood flow on the deck. They stood dumbfounded and silent. The fury of one of the most dangerous men onboard had been snuffed out by the young African.

One of the crewmen whispered, "Just because the river is quiet, don't think the crocodiles have left."

The captain came on deck in time to see the amazing sight. He carried a gun in each hand so he could shoot down the troublemakers. When he saw that the crew had suddenly stopped fighting because of Sammy, he knew that this African boy had an unusual power. It was stronger than the cruelest of men onboard. What power did that Kru possess? How did he manage to bring peace to such a volatile moment? He beckoned Sammy to follow him back to his cabin.

The captain's cabin had been transformed under Sammy's care. It looked like new, sparkling with cleanliness. "The Spirit will not live where filth remains," Sammy often said as he tackled each job. For years, filth and grime had built up around the room. Sammy had set to work with soap and water. He even turned the deadly weapons hanging on the walls into decorations by polishing them. Now the captain looked around the changed room and realized he needed to be changed as well.

barter with the natives. He felt uneasy about the island, so he armed his men and took a larger crew than usual into the small boat. He instructed the lookout in the crow's nest to scan the shore carefully with his marine glasses and signal him if anything unusual happened.

The boat was lowered into the water. The extra men on board made the boat so heavy that it moved slowly against the tide. The island they were heading for looked peaceful. Suddenly the lookout spotted several light boats being thrust into the water from the beach.

He shouted, "Hundreds of men are carrying light canoes!"

Through his binoculars he watched many natives manning the boats, armed with clubs and knives. Led by a white man, the islanders were bent on capturing the small boat, the ship, and the cargo. Only a few weeks before, they had succeeded in such an attack.

Feverishly, the lookout waved his arms to signal the captain to return to the ship. The heavy-laden boat was difficult to maneuver. They headed back toward the ship, but the weight of the cargo slowed them down. Before the captain and his men could reach their ship, the small boats surrounded them.

The captain ordered his men to open fire. At such a close range, every shot found its mark. Gaining time for a getaway, the boat barely reached the ship before being attacked again. The captain and his men quickly boarded the ship. Now the crew on deck poured fire into the attackers.

The leader and his followers threw rope ladders to

"I want to thank you for preventing a big brawl out there," said the captain. He cleared his throat. "Will you pray for me?" he asked Sammy.

Sammy smiled and knelt with the man who had cursed at him, kicked him, and knocked him unconscious. He helped his captain pray a prayer of repentance. Sammy prayed, "Oh, Father, thank You for overpowering the Malay. Thank You for peace onboard this ship. Dear Father, forgive the captain and make him whole again."

The captain possessed a new heart! He and Sammy prayed that the rest of the crew would come to know the unsurpassing love of Christ. After prayers, Sammy and the captain sang songs and talked. Thinking of the missionaries' custom of giving new believers new names, Sammy told the captain, "I cannot give you a new name for becoming a Christian, but instead I gave you new quarters."

The captain was so pleased with his transformed cabin that he invited the ship's officers to see it. In his cabin, they heard testimonies and sang songs. Mysteriously a Bible appeared on a table, and the captain read parts of Scripture.

Gradually, Sammy won the captain's heart completely. At first he had been annoyed by Sammy's frequent prayers; now he stood silently, cap in hand, while Sammy prayed. Under this influence, the captain no longer paid his crew with rum. Serious fights among the crew ceased. Now, the captain would call his crew to quarters for prayers.

On such occasions, Sammy's clear, strong voice and the songs he had learned by heart while in Liberia played a great part in winning the goodwill of the crew. Captain and crew, when off duty, would sit for hours and listen to Sammy sing those beautiful, soul-stirring religious songs, which never lose their power and charm. As Sammy would sing, voice after voice would catch up the melody of the chorus until all would come under the spell of the tender passion of man's eternal quest for God and the sense of wonder at His answering grace.

After one of the meetings, six of the group seemed reluctant to leave.

"Let's go on deck for a while," a German crewman suggested. The sailors climbed the stairs and lounged together in the fading sunset of the open sea. The men exchanged memories of home. The German told a story that made the group laugh together. In the distance, they saw the evening star. The slap, slap of the waves against the side of the ship felt comfortable. A pleasant, warm evening surrounded them.

After a moment of silence, Sammy said, "Your story makes me think of a saying we have in Africa, 'Fair speech turns elephants away from the garden path.' "

A Bulgarian added, "We say, 'Gentle words open iron gates.' "

"We say, 'Ask me what is my virtue, not what is the color of my skin,' " a Middle Eastern crewman added.

The German laughed. "I see you got the point of my story. In Germany we say, 'You should not hate everyone who has a different nose than you.' "

Everyone in the group had spoken but the Slovak, who now offered, "You know I'm a loner, but this cruise has

been different. I've learned the truth from my country, 'A handful of friends is better than a wagon of gold.' " A feeling of kinship grew among the crew as more sailors accepted a personal relationship with Jesus Christ.

The crew continued their travel along the coast of Africa. The influence of the Lord's presence began to change the atmosphere on the ship. The captain summoned crew members to the cabin for prayers. Sammy's constant singing of the hymns he learned became contagious. The sailors started joining in whenever they had the chance. Rum was no longer offered as reward. Peace began to reign.

A few days later, the crew reported, "The Malay is dangerously ill. All hope of recovery is gone."

When Sammy heard this news, he rushed to the Malay's bunk. There he stayed, cooling the cruel man's hot forehead and praying. His prayers were answered and the Malay recovered. Though he could speak little English and Sammy knew nothing of the Malay language, he conveyed to Sammy that he would protect him with his very life.

"Don't give your life to me, give it to Jesus," Sammy pleaded. "God healed you, not me." The Malay didn't understand, but he followed Sammy everywhere.

Several days later the captain announced to the crew, "Only a few more stops and we will be ready to steer straight for New York."

The ship's hold was nearly full of cargo. The captain decided on one last stop. The next morning the captain decided to go ashore with a stock of merchandise

the rail of the ship and climbed aboard. "Surrender the ship or die!" the leader shouted.

The ship's crew had had time to climb high up on the rigging. One of these men shot the leader. A few of his followers, however, dashed for the hatch and reached the hold of the ship.

Sammy stood by the captain's side when the renegade white man was shot. "Sammy," ordered the captain, "go to my cabin, lock and bolt the door on the inside, and guard the ship's valuables. And pray, boy, pray!"

Sammy hurried to obey, but his chest pounded with fear. Memories of the murderous attacks of the Grebos flooded his mind. He ran to the cabin. Quickly he locked up the captain's valuables and bolted the door behind him.

The crew moved to lock their attackers inside the hold. Then they turned their attention to the swarms of islanders still coming over the sides of the ship. The fighting on deck reached a feverish pitch. The attackers managed to swarm the deck like driver ants. Gunfire punctuated the air again and again. Shouts and cries of agony exploded from the throats of those who were cut down by bullets or knives.

Locked in the captain's quarters, Sammy couldn't see the fighting, but he heard everything. It was a fight to the death, and Sammy fell on his knees and prayed, "Oh, Father, do something. Stop this horror, please, Father." He poured out his heart in intercession for his friends.

Finally, about midday, a stiff breeze blew in and pitched the boat. The heavy rocking of the ship prevented any more islanders from climbing aboard. The

91

captain and his men fought fiercely and defeated their attackers. The roar of battle diminished and gave way to somber silence.

"Thank You, Father. Praise Your holy name," Sammy continued to pray. Then he heard the click, click of the anchor chains. The ship moved. For hours he listened to the tramp of heavy-booted feet on the deck. Then he heard the splash of dead bodies being thrown into the sea.

At nightfall, Sammy heard the crew unlock the hatches. The pirates locked in the hold with the rum had drunk so much that they were easily overcome.

Finally, Sammy heard a knock on his door. "Let me in. This is the captain."

Quickly Sammy opened the door. The captain swaggered into the room more dead than alive. He was completely exhausted from loss of blood and the long, terrific struggle. He sank to the floor in a faint. Sammy pulled the big man onto his bunk then tore away the captain's clothes and washed his wounds. When the exhausted man awoke, he found his wounds bandaged and Sammy praying. Gently the captain put his arms around Sammy's shoulders and drew him closer.

"Sammy! Your prayers have saved us and the ship. Although our men fought with courage, we were outnumbered ten to one. Few of our attackers had guns, but they all had knives or war clubs. If the wind had not sprung up so that the ship rolled, the attackers would have swarmed over us like ants. We should have lost! We are safe now."

Sammy urged the captain to rest. Then he went above

to see who else was wounded and needed care. When Sammy emerged on deck, the sight that met his eyes was devastating. The stain of blood was everywhere. Body after body continued to be thrown overboard.

Sammy grieved as he watched those whom he had come to know as friends fall to their watery grave. To the living, Sammy became physician, nurse, and comforter throughout the remainder of the voyage. His cheerfulness and his complete faith in God's Providence soon transformed the ship. Everyone went about their tasks willingly and without the usual curses and beatings.

Sammy's gentle hands dressed their wounds. His caring heart and joyful voice lightened the spirits of the entire crew. The Light of the World shone through Samuel Morris, lighting the dark and lonely corners of many of the sailors' hearts.

six

In the days that followed the battle, the crew buried their friends at sea and life returned to a peaceful state. The men took a greater interest in spiritual matters and crowded the prayer meetings in the captain's cabin. The arguments between the men disappeared, and the remainder of their trip to America was pleasant.

Sammy kept busy caring for the wounded and cleaning the ship. He didn't know what was ahead for him when he arrived in New York. He knew that he would look for Stephen Merritt and learn more about the Holy Ghost. In faith, Sammy continued praying that his heavenly Father would guide his steps to Mr. Merritt.

Suddenly Sammy heard the lookout call out, "There it is! Land! New York!" He rushed on deck to the side of the captain. The captain pointed out a huge statue of a woman with a raised torch on the edge of the harbor. It was the Statue of Liberty.

"You are now at liberty to search for your Mr. Merritt," the captain said. "You've earned your passage with your good work on the ship. Thank you, Sammy."

Sammy was completely overcome with emotion when the harbor was sited. Hardships and suffering were forgotten. Everyone aboard the ship was now his friend, and the once bloodthirsty Malay was the fondest crew member of all.

The ship docked in New York Harbor. Then the crew pulled together some clothing for Sammy and said their good-byes. As they shook hands with Sammy for the last time, many of these hardened men wept like children. Racial barriers were forgotten; they had found a bond of affection stronger than the accident of birth. God's dark-skinned ambassador had dwelt among them. Through him, they had come to realize that there is a personal, prayer-answering God who is no respecter of race or color.

When Sammy had come onboard the ship in Africa, all of his belongings could be gathered in a little piece of handkerchief. When the ship arrived at New York Harbor, he had a sailor's bag full of clothing and presents from the crew. He landed without a cent in his pocket, without friends to greet him or a home to go to. But such matters presented no concerns for Samuel Morris when he walked down the gangplank. He was on a mission to find Stephen Merritt. After almost six months on the ship, he reached the huge city where large buildings rose above the harbor like a bustling crowd. Sammy had never before seen so many buildings in one place.

It was Friday, Sammy's original Deliverance Day, when the ship docked on the East River. The late afternoon sun cast a golden hue over the city. The water rushed smoothly toward the dock, lapping its sides and breaking away again with swaying rhythm. Samuel had one goal in mind—find Stephen Merritt. He called to an ill-dressed man he saw walking past the wharf. The man didn't seem to be going anywhere.

"Sir, where can I find Stephen Merritt?"

"It be Stephen Merritt that you are wanting? As a matter of fact, I do know him," the stranger responded.

Of the many people in New York City, Samuel had located a homeless person who had been to Bethel Mission, a ministry run by Stephen Merritt. This man, a confirmed drunkard, had apparently made the rounds to some of New York's churches and missions begging for money.

Stephen Merritt was unknown near New York Harbor because his mission was three miles from the port. If the Holy Ghost had not guided Samuel Morris to ask the homeless man for directions, it would have been impossible for Sammy to locate Merritt in the thousands of people who lived in New York City.

"Please take me to him," Sammy begged the homeless man.

"Not so fast, young man. We're standing on Pike Street and the mission is way over on Eighth Avenue. I'll take you there for a dollar."

Samuel agreed to the price, even though he had no money. He offered a quick prayer to his heavenly Father that God would continue to meet his physical and financial needs. He followed the man through the streets of New York. He was amazed at the large number of people, the tall buildings, and the garbage in the streets.

Finally they arrived on Eighth Avenue and saw a man unlocking a door. His guide pointed, "That man at the door is Stephen Merritt." Merritt was then the pastor of the St. James Street Methodist Episcopal Church. When Sammy arrived, Merritt was just leaving for a prayer meeting.

Sammy ran forward and began talking with the man. "Mr. Merritt, I am Samuel Morris. I have just come from Africa to learn about the Holy Ghost!"

Mr. Merritt smiled at the young black man and asked, "Do you have any letters of introduction from your church leaders?"

"No, I did not have time to wait for these letters," Sammy said. "I came as fast as I could."

Stephen Merritt smiled at the eagerness of the young man. "I have to go to a meeting just now," Mr. Merritt explained. "I do not have time to talk to you now. Go into the mission next door and wait. I will give you food and a place to sleep for the night."

Samuel agreed to wait and headed for the mission. Then his guide complained about his money. Sammy said, "Stephen Merritt pays all my bills now."

Mr. Merritt smiled at his new student. "Certainly," he said, handing the man a dollar, and climbed into his coach. Sammy nodded his appreciation. As Mr. Merritt drove off, the experienced teacher wondered what the young African would bring into his life.

It was after eleven o'clock when Mr. Merritt returned to his home that evening. He had been delayed partially because his prayer meeting had such extraordinary

97

spiritual intensity that nearly everyone was oblivious about the time. Several times in the past, Mr. Merritt had been arrested for keeping the meeting open at a late hour. The judge had released Mr. Merritt with the understanding that he was to close his meetings in the mission at eleven o'clock sharp.

After Stephen Merritt finished his prayer meeting, he took his carriage home. As he started to step out of his carriage, he remembered the African boy and called his driver to take him back to Bethel Mission. When Mr. Merritt returned to the mission, he had the surprise of his life.

The young black man was kneeling on the platform of the mission. Seventeen men were on their faces, on the floor surrounding Sammy. They were weeping and praying in repentance. Sammy had shared his testimony of God's grace and salvation. The power of God fell on the men and they cried out to God. The scene played out the truth of Jesus' words found in John 6:44: "No one can come to me unless the Father who sent me draws him."

Merritt was stunned. This young man, with virtually no education or training, had led nearly twenty people to Christ on his first day in America! In fact, this boy could barely speak English. Merritt immediately knew that only God could have empowered Samuel Morris and sent him to the United States.

After the meeting, Mr. Merritt said to Sammy, "Come home with me." They left a student preacher surrounded by inquirers. Outside the mission, Sammy marveled that they were to ride in such a fine coach.

"What beautiful horses!" Sammy exclaimed. He was fascinated by the beautiful team of horses that pulled the carriage, and he couldn't take his eyes off them.

"What makes the lights shine on the streets?" Sammy asked.

"They are gas lights," Stephen Merritt answered.

"Gas? That is a new word for me. At home we only have one eye of the night," Sammy explained.

"Never mind. We must get you to bed. It's very late."

Stephen Merritt was a wealthy man and lived in a large home in Hoboken Heights. It was one o'clock in the morning when they reached his residence.

When they arrived at the Merritt home, Sammy wanted to stay in the carriage house with the horses. "I can sleep in the hay," he pointed out.

"Oh, no. You are sleeping in the bishop's bed tonight," Mr. Merritt insisted as he led Sammy to the kitchen door of his fine home. "You brought the Spirit of God to those men tonight!"

Mrs. Merritt had waited up for her husband. "Why, who have you here, Stephen?" she asked in surprise when she saw the young African standing at her door. The black boy's uncouth features and his unsightly sailor-made garb were enough to startle anyone.

"This is an angel in ebony, Dolly, my dear," replied Mr. Merritt. "Meet Samuel Morris, from Liberia."

"What are you going to do with him?" stammered an astounded Dolly Merritt.

"I'm going to give him the Bishop's room," replied Mr. Merritt.

"Oh, no! Don't do that!" Dolly objected. But Mr. Merritt was bent on his plans for Sammy.

Stephen Merritt led Sammy up to the guest room, which had been set apart as the lodging place for Bishop William Taylor whenever he was in New York. William Taylor was a bishop in the Methodist Episcopal Church.

Sammy had never slept in a real bed before, so Stephen had to show Sammy how to pull back the covers and get into one, as well as how to light the gas and turn it off. He even brought out one of the Bishop's own long nightgowns. Sammy had never worn pajamas before. Mr. Merritt explained to him what to do.

When he came back to check on Sammy, he laughed out loud. Sammy's skinny frame was swallowed up because the Bishop was a large man and his voluminous gown made Sammy look funny. Sammy grinned at his new friend. He reached out his hand.

"When are you going to teach me about the Holy Ghost?" Sammy asked.

"Not tonight, son. It's one o'clock in the morning. Sleep well."

"Let's pray together," suggested Sammy.

They knelt beside the bed. Sammy poured out his heart in thankfulness to God. He thanked God for his marvelous preservation from death at the hands of his cruel captors in Africa and for protection in the jungle. Finally Sammy thanked God for the safe trip to New York and the kindness of this dear man and his wife. His heart rejoiced at the hand of God in his life. There was so much to be thankful for!

The presence of God filled the room as Samuel prayed. Mr. Merritt bowed his head in awe. More than ever he knew this young man was wholly dedicated to God and sent to America for a purpose. For many years, Mr. Merritt had been preaching the gospel of Jesus Christ. He was the man Bishop William Taylor had selected to be his secretary, but Mr. Merritt had never before met God as in those few minutes of prayer with Sammy Morris. That day he received a deeper understanding of his Father.

The next morning, Sammy was missing. Mr. Merritt looked all through the house for his young friend and finally found him in the stables.

"What in the world are you doing here?" Mr. Merritt chided Sammy. "I went to your room and found you gone. I've hunted everywhere!"

"No one was awake, so I came out here to see the horses. The groom was combing them, so I helped," Sammy said. When Mr. Merritt said nothing in response, Sammy added weakly, "I didn't know I was doing anything wrong."

"Oh, it's all right. Come along; Dolly has prepared our breakfast."

Samuel's stomach began to growl at the sound of food. Breakfast sounded great! Unknown to Sammy, he was the first black person to sit at the Merritts' table. As he sat down at the table, Sammy thought of Miss Knolls. *It is good that Miss Knolls taught me how to eat with a fork and spoon and to cut my food with a knife.*

Mr. Merritt dispelled the tension of his family with his easy manner. The food set before them was different from what Sammy ate in his homeland. Dolly blinked when she saw this unattractive young man in his strange clothes sitting in her well-done kitchen. The odd clothes Sammy wore were in strange contrast to the beautifully furnished room and the well-dressed family. Sammy listened as Mr. Merritt asked Dolly to bless the food. He saw her stiff face and heard the little memorized prayer. Somehow he felt uncomfortable.

Mr. Merritt taught Sammy about the types of food in America and the customs of eating. Sammy was a willing and hungry student! Then Mr. Merritt explained that he had to conduct a funeral that morning for a gentleman who had died in Harlem. He wanted to take Sammy along with him.

"Not in those clothes," Dolly protested.

"We can stop for new clothes on the way," Mr. Merritt laughed. "I know what you are thinking, Dolly. 'Man looketh on the outward appearance,' but remember, Dolly, 'The Lord looketh on the heart.'"

Sammy was relieved when they were on their way in the coach.

"I must pick up two other ministers. They can take you shopping for clothes while I run another errand. Then I'll return for you, and we'll still be on time for the funeral."

When the two ministers entered the carriage and saw Sammy, they gave some questioning looks and openly

102

displayed their displeasure at Sammy's presence. Mr. Merritt felt sad when he saw how the two ministers looked at Sammy, so he tried to make him forget the men by pointing out the interesting places they were passing. While Stephen Merritt was on his errand, the ministers enjoyed selecting clothing for Sammy. "I never knew there was such a place!" Sammy exclaimed over the rows and rows of fine sweaters, shirts, and suits.

As Sammy tried on clothing, he stood in front of a mirror and looked at himself. He exclaimed, "Prince Kaboo, I don't know you. I don't even know Sammy Morris." Then he looked for a long minute into the mirror. "But God has given me a new way to look. Thank You, God."

A while later, Mr. Merritt returned to the store. Sammy saw the approval in his eyes at his new appearance. He picked up the many boxes of clothing and walked to the counter to pay the bill. Even Mr. Merritt was surprised at the total. He told the clerk, "Where two or more Methodist preachers are gathered together, they cannot be outdone in generosity when someone else is footing the bill."

The ministers looked at each other and laughed. "You told us, 'Nothing is too good for the boy,' remember. Now he looks like Fifth Avenue. Notice those patent leather shoes. They are the latest fashion."

Sammy saved his old clothes because he knew the sailors had given him these clothes in love. In fact, Mr. Merritt insisted on keeping them in his office. He kept them for many years in his office and showed them to people who came in so they would not forget Sammy.

As they got back into the coach, Mr. Merritt showed Sammy the different points of interest.

"This place is called Central Park," he said. "See the Grand Opera House, and over there, see the magnificent bridge."

"Stephen Merritt," interrupted Sammy, "do you never pray in a coach?"

"Why, yes, I often think on spiritual things while I'm riding along," said Mr. Merritt.

Sammy placed his large black hand over Stephen's white one. "Then we will pray." Samuel knelt down in the coach and pulled Stephen Merritt to his knees also. The other two ministers remained seated but bowed their heads.

Merritt looked in amazement at the young man and wondered what would happen next. He had prayed before in a coach, but never on his knees! The prayer that came forth from Samuel Morris would change Stephen Merritt's life.

"Holy Ghost," said Sammy softly, urgently. "I have come all the way from Africa to talk to Stephen Merritt about the Holy Ghost. Now I am here, he shows me the harbor, the churches, the banks and other things, but does not say one word about You. Take out of his heart the things of the earth, and so fill him with Yourself that he cannot speak or write or talk of anything but You."

The burning presence of the Holy Ghost filled the soul of Stephen Merritt. He prayed as he had never prayed before. Stephen Merritt had been in meetings with missionaries, ministers, and bishops, but he had never felt the burning presence of the Holy Ghost as he did while kneeling in this coach beside a poor, homeless African boy.

Here was a man who had taught others about the Holy Ghost and been prayed for by mighty men of God. But the childlike prayer of this supposedly "uneducated" young man from another country pulled back the veil and showed Stephen Merritt how little he did know. Sammy had come to be taught by Merritt. Instead it was Merritt who learned from the young African.

The other ministers also poured out their hearts to God in prayer. Only a few moments before, these two colleagues of Mr. Merritt had felt ashamed to be riding in the same fine coach with this black boy in his ragged clothing. After his prayer, they began to feel their own spiritual shabbiness.

When the carriage stopped, the ministers and Sammy walked inside the church with a spirit of joy and glory. When Merritt preached at the funeral, it seemed the heavens opened. Old things passed away, and his message of comfort seemed to come from God Himself. The people listened in wonder, not knowing that Merritt was speaking with a new sense of power because he had been with Sammy Morris for a few hours. The message so moved the listeners that three men came forward and knelt at the casket to receive Christ.

Sammy sat among the attendants, glowing with the joy of being in such a blessed place, where life was so gently commemorated at death and where Jesus was glorified. Sammy was filled with joy that the man's soul was now in heaven.

While Sammy took no part in the funeral service, he was profoundly interested. Never in his life had he attended a Christian burial. He remembered the orgies that prevailed at the burial of the dead in his own land. He remembered how, at the suggestion of the witch doctor, innocent victims were sacrificed to appease the angry spirits.

The two ministers stayed at the church to talk further with those who had asked how to become Christians.

Later, Merritt took Sammy in the coach to his office. There he answered Sammy's questions about the Holy Ghost. Sometimes together they searched the Scriptures for answers. As they studied, both felt renewed in knowledge and spirit.

On Sunday, Mr. Merritt invited Sammy to attend Sunday school with him. "I am the superintendent of the school. I would like you to speak to the students."

"I was never in Sunday school before, but all right," Sammy said. "What should I say?"

"Just give your testimony and follow the leading of the Holy Ghost."

"All right," Sammy smiled. "I will speak if the Lord wants me to speak."

They arrived at the church. The assembly was overflowing with young people. Every one of them was white and was laughing and telling jokes. Stephen Merritt introduced the visitor.

"This is Samuel Morris," he explained with a smile.

"He has come from Africa to talk to your superintendent about the Holy Ghost. I have asked him to speak to you this morning about the things of the Lord." The young people laughed because it seemed such a funny thing to do.

Sammy stood before the group and waited until all of the laughter stopped. "I was born a prince," he began his testimony. Slowly and quietly, he told his story. The bell rang for the classes to end, but no one moved. Mr. Merritt left Sammy for a few minutes because there was something in the church he needed to tend to.

Sammy prayed. One by one the young people surrounded Sammy, kneeling and asking God to accept them. When Mr. Merritt returned, Sammy was kneeling on the platform and the altar was crowded with six hundred young people. They were kneeling and weeping in prayer. The room was electric with the power of God.

Stephen Merritt said, "Clearly the Holy Ghost has filled the entire place with His glory!"

"It was his prayer," said one student. "When he began to pray, it turned me inside out. Jesus is working through him!"

The next day, Stephen Merritt made up his mind to make a way for Sammy to go to college. Mr. Merritt explained to Sammy that he felt he could help him most by sending him to Taylor University in Fort Wayne, Indiana.

The university was about six hundred miles west of New York. It was staffed by godly people who could help Sammy grow in his knowledge of the Scriptures.

Sammy agreed to the plan. He wanted so much to return to his own land and teach his people about the Lord.

Mr. Merritt dictated a letter to C. B. Stemen, medical doctor, preacher, and former president of Taylor University. In the letter he said, "I'm sending you a diamond in the rough. Please polish him and send him out to enlighten the world. Let me know if you don't have room." Mr. Merritt knew that at Taylor University, Sammy could further his studies in the Bible. He would be equipped to carry on the ministry God had so obviously called him to.

Dr. Stemen immediately showed the letter Dr. Thaddeus Reade, president of Taylor.

"Merritt says he's a diamond in the rough," explained the Reverend Dr. Stemen. "Probably eighteen years old. Merritt says his church at St. James Street will clothe him and pay for his passage to Indiana."

"And would we be willing to take him in and pay for his education?" echoed Dr. Reade, reading from the letter.

He put the letter on his desk and faced his colleague. "I have longed to help students with no money get a college education." He rubbed his chin. "The university is young and struggling with debt. Can we take on the financial responsibility of this lad from Africa?"

The men prayed together. Both concluded it was the Lord's will to accept the new student. A letter was sent right away. "Send him on," it read. "God will take care of him."

Mr. Merritt shared his plan for Sammy's education with the Sunday school young people. Later a group of the young people approached Mr. Merritt. "We want to help Sammy go to college. We've formed the Samuel Morris Missionary Society. The idea is to raise up money for all he needs for school—money, clothes, and books."

Mr. Merritt wholeheartedly supported their efforts. In the days ahead, the young people were able to gather three large trunks, which contained everything Sammy would need to go to Taylor University.

Dolly Merritt was one of the Sunday school teachers. No one was more eager than she to help Sammy, but not because she liked Sammy. She wanted him to be gone from her house.

At Sunday dinner, Dolly asked Sammy to give thanks. Overcome with the kindness of everyone, Sammy expressed his gratitude to his heavenly Father. His simple prayer moved Dolly to tears. The prejudice and reserve in her heart was wiped away. After dinner, Mrs. Merritt put her arm around the black boy. "Our home is yours, Sammy. Whatever we have we will share with you. Stay with us as long as you like."

By the middle of the following week, however, Sammy was ready to take his trip to Fort Wayne, Indiana. After loving good-byes from his friends in New York, Sammy was suddenly alone on the train and looking out the window at the passing scenery.

He wasn't afraid of college. He had no idea what it could be like. As he looked out the window of the speeding train, he was impressed with the mountains, the many cities, the roads, and the carriages. *This place is so different from Africa!*

109

The brief visit from Samuel Morris to New York City proved to be a tremendous blessing to the members of the St. James Street Church. No less than ten thousand people made a personal commitment to Jesus Christ from that time to the end of Stephen Merritt's pastorate. These conversions might not have occurred apart from the spiritual impact of the "Angel in Ebony," as Sammy was called.

The St. James Street Church had known about Christianity in relationship to the human soul and the world, but it wasn't until they saw the poor but earnest figure of Sammy Morris that they understood the reality of their faith. This African pointed them toward the Way, the Truth, and the Life in Jesus Christ.

Several years later, Stephen Merritt wrote about the influence of Sammy Morris on his life: "Bishops have placed their hands on my head once and again, and joined with elders of the church in ordaining services, but no power came in comparison. James Caughey placed his holy hands on my head and on the head of dear Thomas Harrison as he prayed that the mantle of Elijah might fall upon the Elishas—and the fire fell and the power came; but the abiding Comforter was received in the coach with Samuel Morris—for since then I have not written a line or spoken a word, or preached a sermon only for or in the Holy Ghost."

Samuel Morris was never forgotten by the people in the St. James Street Church in New York City.

Sammy Morris continued on his train journey to Fort

110

Wayne, Indiana. The train pulled into the station on Friday, which was Sammy's Deliverance Day or day of fasting and prayer. The president of Taylor University, Thaddeus C. Reade, met Sammy at the train station.

"Welcome, Samuel Morris. Welcome to Taylor University and Fort Wayne!" He smiled and extended his hand.

Sammy gladly took the hand. His eyes sparkled, and he said, "I see why everyone wears so many clothes here. It's cold!"

"You've not seen anything yet, Sammy. Just wait until winter gets here. You will learn a new meaning for the word 'cold.' "

President Reade liked the young man but kept wondering what to do with him. Obviously he wasn't ready for college work. Together they located Sammy's three luggage trunks, and two students placed them on a wagon. When the loading was finished, Sammy and the president took the coach to the school.

On the way, the president asked Sammy about the kind of room that he wanted.

"If there is a room nobody wants, then give that one to me," Sammy said.

Dr. Reade turned away from the boy to hide the tears that sprang from his eyes. The humility and sincerity of this new student pierced the heart of the college president. Over the years, he had assigned rooms to over a thousand students. Most of them were young Christian ladies and gentlemen. Not one had ever offered to take a room no one else would take!

111

I was asking myself whether I would be willing to take what nobody else wanted. The Holy Ghost was at work in my heart the minute I met Sammy, Dr. Reade thought.

seven

The next morning, Sammy woke up with a sinking feeling. He looked around his bare dorm room and thought, *I have books that I can't read and more clothes than I can ever wear. I'm just a poor, ugly, black boy in an all-white college.* He leaped out of bed and flung himself on his knees next to his bed.

"Father, oh, Father, why do You want me here? I do want to serve You among my people, but Africa seems so far away. Please help me to lean on the Holy Ghost this day!"

Suddenly a bell rang, and Sammy could hear running feet and shouting. When he answered a knock on his door, he saw a young man with freckles and the brightest red hair that he had ever seen. "I'm Eddie from next door. Dr. Reade asked me to help you get started."

Sammy grinned. "I guess I need help. Thanks, Eddie."

"Be ready in ten minutes. Breakfast is at eight o'clock."

Sammy looked confused and said, "Ten minutes? What's ten minutes?"

Eddie looked at his new friend. "Oh, boy, you do

need help! They say, 'A friend in need is a friend indeed.' Do you have a clock?"

With a shrug Sammy said, "I have trunks of stuff—somewhere."

"They are outside your door. If you give me a hand, we will unpack after breakfast," Eddie said. "But now, Sammy Morris, you wash up and put on your clothes—fast—that will take ten minutes."

Sammy knew what the word *fast* meant. He was ready before Eddie returned to his room.

The dining room at Taylor University was bigger than anything Sammy could imagine. He thought that he could slip into the room and eat breakfast without any-one noticing, but many of the students stared at the young black man.

"I don't think they like me," Sammy said to Eddie as he looked around the room.

"They don't know you. They stare at any new stu-dent who enrolls after school begins," Eddie explained.

After breakfast, the pair transformed Sammy's room. Sammy began to understand why he needed the things in each of his three trunks. They hung curtains, put down throw rugs, and arranged his bedding. In addition, they hung Sammy's clothes in the closet and arranged his books on the desk. Eddie showed him how to start and turn off the gas lights. "Be sure you light them every time you turn on the gas," he said. "Gas is poison unless it's burning."

Poison. What's poison? Sammy wondered. While he understood English, there were many new words to learn.

114

Eddie tried to speak with small words, but still was surprised at some of the words Sammy didn't understand.

That afternoon President Reade also learned what Sammy didn't know. He realized that the new student couldn't fill out the application form. "I'll just enroll you as a special student," he said kindly. "Eddie, take Sammy to the ball game this afternoon and to church tomorrow. Monday morning, take him to registration, and I'll handle things from there."

While Sammy didn't know it, Dr. Reade called together a group of professors and school officials for a meeting. "We have a problem," he began. "Sammy can't read or write or understand enough for college work. What can we do?"

One professor said, "It's simple; send him away. The French have a saying, 'There's no way to change a buzzard into a hawk.'"

"Wait just a minute," Dr. Parker offered. "I know Stephen Merritt, and he would not have sent Sammy to our school if he had no potential."

The treasurer added his opinion. "Hey, this isn't a charity school. You know how we have to skimp on our meals because we don't have enough funds. Why are we adding to our financial burden? I say if the boy can't pay his way like the other students, then we don't need him."

"Dr. Parker," the president said, "I'm going to ask you to interview Sammy and set up a course of study for him. Perhaps some of the students, when they learn of his need, will give free tutoring lessons."

"What about his money?" the treasurer asked in a bitter voice.

"I will be personally responsible," Dr. Reade said. "I'm speaking at a church next Sunday and will make an appeal for funds."

"Then I'll send his bills to you, Mr. President!"

On that sour note, the meeting ended. Only Professor Parker seemed to be happy with the challenge that he had been given to direct Sammy's program.

Before Sammy's arrival, Dr. Reade had lengthy discussions about him with one of Fort Wayne's distinguished citizens, Dr. Christian B. Stemen. This honored physician had been a previous president of the college.

Dr. Stemen encouraged Dr. Reade to accept Sammy into the college because Stephen Merritt had told him that Sammy's arrival would mean a spiritual blessing to the school and an asset to the life of the student body as a whole. When Sammy arrived, Dr. Stemen took a great interest in Sammy. He saw this as his opportunity to realize, at least in part, his early dreams of investing his life as a medical missionary to Africa.

However, Dr. Reade enrolled Sammy with a heavy heart. He could see no talent in this unattractive black boy; he could only see a financial burden that was already too great for the university. Taylor University was on the verge of closing its doors because of a shortage of funds that was so severe that even food for the students was in scarce supply. Involuntary fasting was much in evidence. Dr. Reade, always a man of action, battled daily to keep the university open.

At chapel service, a call was made for volunteers to tutor the new student. Before he could take regular college classes, Sammy needed to be tutored in the basics of a high school education. Several people volunteered. They subsequently found that working with Samuel Morris proved to be a real blessing. He worked hard. He was especially good at studying Scripture.

While Sammy and the other students pursued their studies, Dr. Reade worked hard to keep the university financially afloat. Times were hard for the college. The next Sunday, Dr. Reade spoke at a Methodist Church in Churubusco, just outside of Fort Wayne, Indiana. He appealed to the congregation with a story about their newest student, the young man from Africa.

"This boy named Sammy Morris has arrived from Africa without a penny to pay for his food. I took him on as a student in faith that someone would give the money to educate him." Then Dr. Reade asked people to give financial aid to support Samuel Morris's education.

After the service, Dr. Reade stood at the rear door and shook hands. Mr. Thomas was the only person that morning who gave something for Samuel Morris—fifty cents. The meager results were extremely discouraging to Dr. Reade. But on his way to catch his train, a man called to him from inside a butcher shop. It was Josiah Kichler. He handed Dr. Reade a five-dollar bill.

"I heard your appeal for that poor black boy. The Holy Ghost tells me to give this to your faith fund," said the butcher. Dr. Reade thanked him and boarded his train.

Instead of being discouraged, his heart rang with

hope. Faith fund. The words resounded in the college president's ears. "We shall have a Samuel Morris Faith Fund," decided Dr. Reade. "All contributions shall be used to help Sammy get the education that he needs."

Samuel objected. "The fund should not be for me. That is God's money. I want you to use it for other students who are more worthy than I."

But the fund proved to be part of God's plan. Contributions started to come in on a regular basis. Sammy insisted that Dr. Reade use the money to pay only for his necessities. He never put a penny in his own pocket. Within ten years of the establishment of this fund, enough money had been contributed for more than two hundred students to receive help in their struggle for an education.

Dr. Reade continued to work on raising funds for Samuel Morris and others in the school. Shortly after Sammy's arrival on campus, Dr. Reade wrote about Sammy in the *Western Christian Advocate*. He invited anyone who felt moved to do so to send a dollar each toward Sammy's expenses. Thirteen people responded, and their funds were used to fix up Sammy's room and buy his books.

At Monday morning chapel, three days after Sammy's arrival, Dr. Reade told the students about Sammy. He even asked for volunteers to teach the new student. "If you would like to help in the education of this angel in ebony, then see Dr. Parker after lunch," he said. Sammy wasn't in the chapel to hear this request.

Eddie had left Sammy in the registration department

as instructed. Sammy sat on a bench in the hall. He was fascinated with the walnut paneling, the colored glass above the doors, and the polished brass gas fixtures. He was especially interested in the brass knocker on the door of the registrar's office. He stepped up to it and found he could lift it. When he let go, it landed on the door with a great clatter. The door opened and a prim lady appeared. "And what is your business?" she asked.

Sammy was speechless, so the woman returned to her office. After the woman shut the door, Sammy returned to his seat and soon bowed his head and began to pray. He determined that he didn't like brass knockers.

Later Dr. Reade arrived, apologizing for being so late. "And now I must leave you again while I talk to the registrar for a minute." Sammy didn't know much about time, but it seemed much longer than a minute to him before the president returned.

Dr. Reade came back with Professor Parker, who took Sammy into a small room. On a table was a large stack of books. Sammy tried to read from several of them before he found one that was easy for him. "Good! Good!" Dr. Parker seemed pleased. "We'll begin there." While Sammy was about eighteen, in his academic learning he was like a child of seven or eight. The only solution was a long period of private instruction through tutors so that he could catch up on his education.

As Sammy and Dr. Parker continued to look through the stacks of books, they located a spelling and writing book like the ones Mrs. Davis had used on the coffee plantation in Africa. "Ho, I know where I left off in this

119

book," Sammy said as he pointed to a page.

"Good, good!" Dr. Parker agreed.

When they looked through the arithmetic books, it was a different story. It seemed that neither Mrs. Davis nor the missionaries had taught Sammy anything beyond simple addition and subtraction. "That's all right; we have an excellent math teacher," Dr. Parker reassured Sammy.

Finally, they spoke about the Bible, and Sammy's face lit up. This was a topic that he knew something about! By the end of the day, Sammy knew his class schedule. His courses were in reading, writing, and arithmetic. Besides these, Sammy took a class in spelling. The only class that he attended with the university students was Bible. He didn't take notes or tests, but he so enjoyed the study of the Word of God.

Eddie and Sammy were becoming close friends. Eddie showed Sammy how to use an alarm clock and how to read time.

"Why is everything in a day related to time?" Samuel asked.

"Well, they serve meals at 8:00 a.m., 12:00 noon, and 6:00 p.m. If you think time doesn't matter, you will starve." Eddie laughed. "Classes also meet at certain times." But Sammy lost interest in time and changed the topic of conversation.

"Eddie, is there no place around here where black people have church?" Sammy asked. "I saw in New York that black people had a different church than white people."

"Yes, the black people here have a nice church, and

it's only about ten blocks from the college," Eddie said.

"Blocks? What are blocks?"

Eddie was getting pretty accustomed to Sammy's questions about unfamiliar words. He didn't recall explaining the word *block* to him before. "You know the streets your carriage followed to bring you from the railroad station to the school?"

"Oh, yes, the path; we also have paths in Africa."

"Well, the ground between the paths is called a block. So you walk ten blocks on East Wayne Street, and you are at the church."

Sammy looked puzzled. "You mean you cross ten paths?"

"Yes, but let me take you to East Wayne Street, so you will know where to begin counting."

The friends walked past the college entrance, and Eddie showed Sammy the sign that said "East Wayne."

"I can find it now, I think," Sammy said, "but it doesn't look *down* to me. It looks straight ahead."

Eddie was surprised. "I guess I did say *down* the street. Just forget it because it doesn't slope in a downward direction." Eddie had no idea why he had used the word down, but it was a natural part of the English language.

On the way back to the dorm, Eddie showed Sammy the different buildings and explained their names. Sammy began to wonder if he would ever understand this strange world.

When they returned to his room, Sammy asked Eddie, "Please help me light this gas light. This room is beautiful. It's as nice as the bishop's room in New York."

121

"You slept in the bishop's room? I thought his room was kept for him alone."

"I don't know," Sammy said. "That's where the Holy Ghost took me. I keep wondering what the Holy Ghost will do next!"

Eddie turned to his new friend and gave him a strange look. "I'm a Christian, too, Sammy, but I never think about the Holy Ghost."

"You should!" Sammy followed Eddie to the door. They said good night, and Eddie went to his room, wondering why he had never talked with his heavenly Father the way Sammy talked with Him.

Despite Eddie's instruction about the new clock, Sammy was still late for church. He didn't know it would take so much time to walk ten blocks. When he arrived at the church service, all of the singing and prayers were over. Every seat was covered with a starched white doily, as were the arms of each seat. The members of the choir were in black robes and had just been seated. Everything was in perfect order for the service.

Sammy walked down the aisle to the church as the minister stood from his chair and announced his text to the congregation. Instead of taking a seat, Sammy mounted the platform and spoke to the minister. "I am Samuel Morris, and I've just arrived from Africa. I have a message for your people."

"Do you have a sermon prepared?" the minister asked, thinking that Sammy was a preacher.

Sammy looked the minister straight in the eye. His

face shone with a strange light and he said, "No sermon, but I have a message!"

The minister looked with surprise at the new visitor. He was a strict disciplinarian and set in his ways. Sammy's boldness was very disconcerting to him, but there was something about the young man that prompted the minister to accede to his request. The minister sat down by the collection table with a puzzled expression. Sammy began not by preaching, but by talking with his Father. Suddenly the church was filled with commotion as people got on their knees, weeping, praying, and shouting for joy.

Afterward, the minister said, "I did not listen to what he was saying. I was seized with an overpowering desire to pray. What I said and what Sammy said I do not remember, but I know my soul was on fire as never before. The power that brought Samuel Morris out of bondage in Africa was shining in our hearts in Fort Wayne. Our people had never before seen such power of the Holy Ghost."

Revival had come to the church on East Wayne Street. The meeting carried on long after the allotted time. The people basked in the presence of the Lord. When the people finally left for their homes, they realized Samuel Morris had spoken the language of the human soul. He had appealed to their heavenly Father from the depths of his own soul. His intercession had been uttered in absolute faith, and the Spirit was there in answer to that childlike faith. Everyone went home rejoicing.

To everyone's surprise, the local newspapers heard

of the event and printed editorials. Many other papers copied and printed the story. Almost overnight, Samuel Morris, the new African student at Taylor University, became a household name in the city of Fort Wayne!

On campus, Sammy's walk with God excited his fellow students. His joy in learning, his simple faith, his powerful prayers—these all turned the eyes of student and staff alike to examine their own relationships with God. In the hands of God, Samuel Morris became a missionary to the students and faculty of Taylor University.

Curiosity about Sammy Morris was great on the Taylor University campus. Once the teacher in the art department asked Sammy to pose in the studio so her students could draw an African. Sammy surprised this teacher with a frank refusal. He said, "I can't stand to be in this room because it is full of strange white heads, white hands, and white feet."

The startled teacher responded, "Sammy, these models are made from plaster and are white because the materials are white."

"It doesn't make any difference to me," Sammy said firmly "I dread to be in the same room with those models."

"What if we used a different room? Then would you be willing to pose for us?" the teacher suggested.

"Yes, that would be fine," Sammy said. So the teacher moved her class to the room across the hall from the studio. There Samuel patiently posed until they completed an excellent portrait of him.

Once Sammy met his teachers and memorized his

class schedule, he felt better. Here was work he could do, and there were pleasant people to help him. Dr. Harriet Macbeth, the daughter of Dr. Christian B. Stemen, was his overall teacher and friend. A member of the Taylor faculty, Dr. Idora Rose, volunteered to help Dr. Macbeth. Sammy truly benefitted from this team-teaching effort.

Samuel Morris was a diligent student. Every word, every thought, every principle that was taught was indelibly fixed in his mind. The refined expressions and the musical accents of his teachers' voices were transferred to his own conversation.

Yet Sammy remained original in his thinking. His grouping of words into sentences was a wonder to all. His sentences were short, but every word in them had meaning. Idle talk was unknown to Sammy. High ideals and noble purposes were his very existence.

Dr. Macbeth soon learned that the burden she had volunteered to carry was to become a well-rewarded labor of love. Every day brought new blessings to his teacher.

But Sammy continued to regard the divine Spirit of Truth as his chief instructor. Often in solving a difficult arithmetic problem, he would say in a low voice, "Lord, help!" He spent more time talking to his Father than any earthly teacher. The Holy Ghost brought God close to Sammy and made Him just as real as any of his college teachers.

One day in the little library room, Dr. Macbeth exclaimed, "Oh, Sammy you are driving yourself to exhaustion studying so hard!"

Sammy looked up from his arithmetic and said, "I know it is hard, but 'nothing falls into the mouth of a sleeping fox.' I must try to catch up. I looked at some of Eddie's books and saw how far ahead of me that he is." Sammy felt desperate to bring his academics on a par with the other students. But it was lonely working in the little room off the library.

He was not alone for long, however. Shortly after Sammy's arrival at Taylor, a Dr. Walker from New York wrote about a young Armenian boy whose mother was a Christian in Turkey. This young man had come to America so he could be educated to help his mother in the work of spreading the gospel of Jesus Christ to their people. He landed in Castle Garden without a friend or a dollar and with very little knowledge of English.

Dr. Walker immediately thought of sending him to Taylor University. The Samuel Morris Faith Fund made it possible for the college authorities to accept this Armenian boy. One day Harriet Macbeth brought a dark-skinned boy with her into the room. "Sammy, this is Aman. He will be studying with us."

Sammy jumped up from his desk and extended his hand to Aman. "Are you a Christian?" he asked.

"Ah, yes, I am a believer. My mother is a Bible woman in Turkey. She prays for me to be a holy man of God." Aman smiled as he put his hand in his pocket.

"And you? Do you also pray?" Sammy asked.

"Ah, yes. My voice rises like a fountain day and night."

"Then let us pray together," Sammy proposed. The

three knelt as each talked to the heavenly Father. Aman prayed, "Let this prayer of devotion, deep in my soul, rise silent to Thee."

Sammy blinked. He wondered, *Will we be friends?* By the end of the week, however, Aman said, "My love is now thawed."

Sammy took Aman's hand and laughed. "Friend, my love was never frozen. I may not always understand you, but I like you."

Aman answered, "Misunderstandings between friends only make the friendship stronger."

They learned to care for each other even when their views seemed worlds apart. Sammy showed Aman around the campus and explained things to him. Together they attended prayer meetings. Like Sammy, Aman also had difficulty with the clock and time. Sammy explained the concepts to him, just as Eddie had done for Sammy. When Sammy finished, Aman said, "I see the finger of the clock runs a circuit, but is still at home."

"Yes, but while it runs, it runs you—to meals, to chapel, to class, and to prayer meetings. Do you understand?" Aman found it easier to wait for Sammy to take him places.

Because Taylor University now had two foreign students, they hired Miss Grace Husted, Dr. Reade's daughter, to help teach the boys. She became a living inspiration to her two pupils.

Speaking about Sammy Morris, Miss Husted wrote, "He was remarkable for his earnest effort to learn and his undivided attention to every lesson. Having nothing to unlearn, possessing no undue conception of his own importance, he was entirely submissive to the instruction and discipline of the teachers.

"It was a delightful period in the days of the class work routine, when he entered the class alone, as he was not sufficiently advanced to recite with the other students. For his English lessons, the Bible was the textbook. Reverently and carefully would he read the chapters assigned. He was so interested in asking questions and in commenting upon the meaning of the text, that the recitation hour was never long enough to satisfy him."

One Sunday, Dr. Stemen took Sammy to Columbia City so he could talk with the people who were interested in the work of Taylor University about Sammy's need. After Dr. Stemen spoke, they collected a freewill offering of eleven dollars.

Sammy didn't know the amount of the offering but turned to Dr. Stemen and whispered in a subdued voice of pain, "Take me where they speak about Jesus." At the words, his physician friend brushed a tear from his eye. Sammy struck the keynote of Christ's teaching found in Matthew 6:33: "Seek ye first the kingdom of God and his righteousness, and all these things shall be added unto you."

After Sammy got to know Aman and a friendship began to thrive between them, Sammy began to think about Henry O'Neill. He prayed for Henry so much that Aman also prayed.

"Why do you pray for this one to come to America?" Aman asked one day.

"Because Henry wants to be a missionary and is smarter than I am," Sammy said.

"What will you do about it?" Aman asked.

The question haunted Sammy. He had trouble sleeping and continued to be deeply troubled. Early one morning Sammy entered Dr. Reade's office with a surprising request.

"May I speak with you, sir?" Sammy began.

"Why yes, Sammy, do come in." Dr. Reade considered Sammy one of his best friends. "How can I help you?" he asked.

"Is it all right if I stop studying for a while and go to work?" Sammy asked.

"Why, Sammy? I'm surprised because I thought you liked it here."

"I do like it very much, sir, but I want to earn money to bring Henry O'Neill to America. He would be a much better student than I am."

"Oh, you're talking about the young man that you led to the Lord in Monrovia. I remember your telling me about him and his testimony." Dr. Reade recalled his conversations with Sammy.

"Yes, Henry is more deserving than I am. He learns faster and should have an opportunity."

"And what of your opportunity? Will you let it flutter away like a feather on the wind?"

"I don't want to, sir. I just wish Henry O'Neill could have such a chance as I have."

129

"Tell you what," Dr. Reade decided. "Let's pray about it and see what your heavenly Father has to say about your friend. If he ought to come to America, the Lord will open the way."

Dr. Reade also promised to write some letters about Henry. Sammy quickly agreed and disappeared to his room for prayer. The next morning, when he returned to Dr. Reade, it was obvious the answer given was a good one. Sammy's face glowed with happiness.

"Well?" inquired Dr. Reade.

"My Father says Henry will be coming over soon. He is taking care of everything."

Dr. Reade wrote to Mrs. Drake in Illinois. With her husband, they had been missionaries in Africa. Dr. Reade learned that Henry O'Neill had been employed by a certain family in Africa.

Arrangements were already being made to bring Sammy's friend to America, but Henry would not be joining Sammy in Fort Wayne, Indiana. Instead, Henry would study in St. Louis under a Miss Adams, who later sent Henry to another school. He studied there for one year, then returned to Africa and helped his people. Henry was one of the first fruits of Sammy's testimony about Jesus Christ. Sammy's prayers about Henry's education were answered.

Sammy's life in Fort Wayne brought a spiritual blessing to people he met, but it also stirred an interest in foreign missionary service. His presence on the campus of Taylor University gave the students a focus on world evangelism. In Sammy's life the students found an answer to their questions about serving Jesus Christ.

Many times Sammy would walk with some of the students outside the city. During these hours, they exchanged their spiritual experiences and discussed their plans for the future.

To one of these friends, Sammy said, "When I get back to Africa, I will gather the children about me and they will sit on the sand. They will call me father, but I wouldn't care for that, I will tell them of Jesus, and some of them will go away in the bushes, and I will know what that means—they are praying and accepting Jesus Christ. When they return, they will be happy."

Children in his homeland of Africa were the heartbeat for Samuel Morris. It is doubtful that Sammy understood the vast difficulties of evangelizing any nation or people, but instinctively his soul cried out to these children. In light of their innocence and helplessness, he could not be indifferent. To be a father to them—a real father—by loving and helping them was the cry of Sammy's heart. Week in and week out he wove this beautiful dream into his glorious plan of helping people.

eight

D r. Reade wrote in several church papers about Samuel Morris. Because of this news, many visitors came to Taylor University and visited Sammy. Since he was never engaged in worthless conversation, Sammy worked out a plan for these visitors. His plan included three things: Sammy introduced himself; he asked the visitors to read the Bible; and he prayed.

Some people were startled when Sammy said, "I am reading through the Bible but find the words difficult. May I ask you to read where the last person left off?" Sammy always handed the Bible to the visitors and then settled down to listen.

Most visitors were happy to read to Sammy and then carefully mark where they had left off. The students at the university found out about Sammy's routine and stopped into his room for reading and prayer. Soon Sammy had many student friends.

The students at Taylor came to know and love the young man from Africa. In the hall that passed Sammy's room, he could often be heard "talking to his Father."

Late at night, early in the morning, Sammy's passion was to pray. When he prayed, he gave his full attention to the Lord.

Once Dr. Reade passed by Sammy's room. He quietly opened the door. There knelt Sammy, his face lifted toward heaven, much like the boy who knelt in the bunkhouse in Liberia, the boy through whom Sammy discovered prayer.

The influence of Sammy's prayers leaked from his room into the halls of the college. Students were drawn to him. A fellow student, Thomas Newburn, told how he often went to Sammy's room and found him at prayer. Sammy would take no notice if anyone knocked at the door, but would continue his talk with God until he had finished. Then he would go to the door, smiling, and say, "Now, come in; we are done talking for this time."

One day Sammy was shocked when a confirmed atheist visited his room. Even the most savage pagan and idolaters in Kru land believed in some kind of god. Sammy had never met anyone who said, "There is no God," and called himself an atheist.

But there was an atheist on campus who heard all about Sammy. He was not satisfied with what was said in favor of Samuel Morris.

"Oh, I can put that unlearned black to shame," he boasted. "I know every argument and the answer to every Scripture." He asked a friend of Sammy's to take him to Sammy and witness his downfall. Sammy's friend laughed, "Remember Proverbs 25:14, 'Whoso boasteth himself of a false gift is like clouds and wind without rain.' "

When the pair arrived at Sammy's room, he was praying, so they waited in the hall for him. After a long time had passed, Sammy opened his door to the friend and the atheist.

After the introductions, Sammy said, "Please read the Bible where the last person marked." He handed the Bible to the atheist, but the student threw it down on the table, scoffing, "I do not read that book anymore. It is full of love affairs, wars, and a lot of big fish stories. I don't believe a word of it."

Sammy sat still and listened to the atheist talk. Then he rose to his feet and spoke with compassion for the fellow student, "My dear brother, your Father speaks to you, and you do not believe Him? Your Brother speaks, and you do not believe Him? The sun shines, and you do not believe it?"

Sammy paused, then continued, "God wishes to be your Father, Christ is your Brother, the Holy Ghost is your Sun." Extending his hand on the atheist's shoulder, he insisted, "Kneel down and I will pray for you."

The atheist sank down as though his life had crumbled within. But he resisted Sammy's prayers and would not open his mouth. When the prayer was over, he stumbled to the door. Suddenly he felt a stab of pain in his heart, and he fled to his room.

Daily, Sammy, Aman and many of their friends prayed for the atheist. Near the end of the semester, the atheist returned to Sammy's room. Sammy smiled and put his hands on both shoulders of the young man saying, "You are a Christian? That's what you have come to tell me?"

"Yes," the atheist agreed. "I have not been able to eat or sleep or study properly. All I could think of was Jesus dying on the cross for me. My Brother, who loved me *that* much."

Together they knelt, and this one-time scoffer prayed from his heart to his heavenly Father. That student became a preacher and then a bishop.

A number of years later, that same student met one of his old atheistic friends. This friend loved to fight about religion as much as the student once had. There was a strong debate between the two old friends. The atheist became angry and hit the preacher on the head. He fell to the floor as though dead.

When he got up again, the preacher was very angry, but suddenly he thought about Sammy Morris lying on the cabin floor of the ship when he had been knocked down by the captain. *If Samuel Morris could forgive that cruel captain and pray for him,* he thought, *why can't I do the same for this man?*

His anger evaporated, and he got on his knees and began to pray for this friend who had hit him. As he prayed, the other man knelt at his side, put his arm around him, wiped the blood from his face, and asked him to forgive him. It proved that Sammy was right when he practiced what God's Word says in Proverbs 15:1: "A gentle answer turns away wrath, but a harsh word stirs up anger."

When the other students at Taylor heard about the changed life of the former atheist, they came to visit Sammy. Some of them wanted to accept Christ, while

135

others wanted to discuss evolution. Yet others wanted to rededicate their lives to Jesus.

"Some of this so-called science takes away my faith and gives me nothing in its place," one of the students said.

"I've been a Christian since I was a small child, but all I ever thought about was getting things—like power and position. I'm afraid I've been very materialistic," another exclaimed.

Even the red-haired Eddie prayed with Sammy. "Oh, Father, I didn't know You were so real I could talk to You like this. I'll trust You forever."

Sammy's room became a haven for anyone who wanted to walk in the Spirit of God.

As Sammy's reading improved, he found a biography of John Wesley and read it. Then Sammy stopped reading and prayed for all the students and for Taylor University.

Although he didn't know it, Taylor University was struggling with its finances. At one point during this time, some thought the doors to the college would have to be closed. The university needed to move from its campus; there was no place to go. But with the help of the growing Faith Fund and the inspiration of Sammy himself, the board pulled together.

Colonel N. D. Foster said, "But what can we do now? Where can we go? We must move from here soon."

A former student named Lindley J. Baldwin spoke up, "Come to Upland, Indiana. We will receive you with open arms. Gentlemen, I have no authority to enter into a contract with you to that effect, but tomorrow I will go

136

to Upland and telegraph you to come there and get your ten thousand dollars and select your ten acres of land."

"I believe the Samuel Morris Faith Fund will bring in enough money to tide us over during the move," the treasurer suggested.

"I'm going to Sammy's room to pray," said Mr. Baldwin.

Early the next morning, Mr. Baldwin appeared at Sammy's door. "I have come to pray with you," he explained. "Our school is in trouble and in need of our prayers."

Together they knelt and prayed for the much needed ten thousand dollars and ten acres of land. It was an inspiring session with just Sammy, Lindley Baldwin, and the Holy Ghost. When they finished, they both believed the prayer would be answered. Mr. Baldwin quoted Tennyson: "More things are wrought in prayer than this world dreams of."

Sammy held Mr. Baldwin's overcoat as he prepared to leave.

He laughed, "Sammy, you are the Moses that will lead Taylor University into the Promised Land!"

Sammy fought to hide his tears. "I don't feel like a Moses," he admitted.

By two o'clock that same day, the ten thousand dollars had been raised as well as ten acres. Samuel Morris and Taylor University were discussed throughout Upland. A committee was appointed to go at once to Fort Wayne and negotiate a contract with the trustees. The committee visited Sammy and was impressed as much as the people who had known Sammy for a longer period of time. The contract was signed, and the beautiful site for the campus selected.

When the move to Upland was assured, they planned a dedication service. On the platform would be Dr. Reade, Lindley Baldwin, and Samuel Morris. All the dignitaries were to attend, but it was Samuel Morris who was scheduled to give the dedication prayer and preach the sermon.

The leadership of Samuel Morris was felt by the majority of the student body. While most of the students were sincere Christians, this was a period in which there was a weakening of faith among churches and church colleges. The Darwinian theory of evolution seemed to strike at the foundations of biblical authority. The increase of wealth through scientific inventions fostered materialism. No one could imagine the forthcoming economic depressions and worldwide wars that so clearly would demonstrate that impersonal science falls far short of being a substitute for a personal relationship with God through Christ.

At the time, Taylor University was under the control of a ministerial association of the Methodist Episcopal Church and maintained an unusually high spiritual standard of education. Yet the vast majority of the laymen and some clergymen of that denomination had ceased to have more than a nominal faith in the work of the Holy Ghost—as was experienced and proclaimed by the founder of Methodism, John Wesley.

Wesley had taught that the state of pure love and

holiness so often encouraged from the Scriptures can actually be maintained through the cleansing power of the Holy Ghost. Such a blameless life was not free from temptation or power to sin, but the sanctified believer was given the power not to sin because his will had been liberated from the power of evil.

This doctrine of sanctification was certainly the key to Wesley's own amazing powerful leadership and the boldness of his faith. In fact, the dynamic power of all successful evangelism is rooted in the power of a Spirit-filled life. Taylor University, through the life of Samuel Morris, was beginning to discover this life of faith.

Sammy electrified the entire university from the president down to the newest freshman by demonstrating the simplicity and power with which the Holy Ghost can confer the graces of leadership on the humblest person. The whole school was lifted to a higher plane in which the students were not merely "saved" but were also spiritually strengthened to save others.

While everyone waited for the university to move to Upland, the school in Fort Wayne continued as usual. Lessons in the little library room were sometimes dull.

To put a spark into their spelling class, Dr. Macbeth decided to have a spelling match between Sammy and Aman.

"It will give me a chance to shine lovely as light!" Aman smiled quietly.

"What do you mean?" Sammy asked. After six months with Aman, Sammy still had trouble understanding him.

"You do shine with the college as a diamond. This will give me a chance to outshine you!"

"Oh, do you think you will win?" Sammy challenged his friend.

"Ah, yes, I will receive the prize and cause your stubborn knees to bow."

"My stubborn knees?" Sammy said. "Come on, Aman. You know my knees are the first to bow in prayer. How can you call them stubborn?"

"Now, now!" Dr. Macbeth said. "I didn't mean to start anything, and I said nothing about a prize for this contest."

Aman's face fell.

"All right, all right, we will have a prize," Dr. Macbeth amended, and she outlined the spelling contest rules.

Since it was Friday, the schoolroom was locked until Monday morning. Unfortunately, Sammy and Aman forgot their spelling books.

At dinner, Aman remarked, "Oh that I had remembered my spelling book."

"Me, too," Sammy said.

"Perhaps we may lift the window in the classroom and get our books," Aman continued. "Don't you think this is a good approach?"

Sammy looked shocked at the idea. "You mean break into the library? Like we are thieves?"

"No, no, of course not like thieves—like we are students who forgot our books." Aman was surprised at Sammy's objection.

"I would hate to be caught doing such a foolish thing," Sammy laughed.

The boys dropped the subject, but both continued to think about it. It occurred to Aman that he would have an advantage if he studied over the weekend. Accordingly, he set out for the library. After locating his book, he heard the sound of footsteps. Quickly, he closed the window and hid in the darkness.

Sammy slipped into the library and located his book. Cloaked in darkness, the schoolroom looked scary, so Sammy didn't waste any time in climbing out of the window.

Throughout the weekend, Sammy intended to go to Aman's room and study spelling with his friend. However, the student revival meetings consumed his attention and Sammy completely forgot about spelling.

Since the students had been clamoring to hear Sammy's message, Dr. Macbeth and Dr. Reade finally agreed to let him speak at the student rally in the college auditorium. Before the event, Sammy dressed carefully. He clutched his few notes, which were the results of many hours with Dr. Macbeth. On the way to the revival, Sammy stopped at Aman's room. "You're not dressed!" Sammy protested. "You know the meeting starts in fifteen minutes!"

"I'm not going," Aman replied simply. "I have to study."

Hiding his surprise, Sammy nodded and then hurried to the auditorium, which was filled with students.

Eddie grabbed Sammy's arm. "Come to the platform. Dr. Reade has been waiting for you."

On the platform, Sammy looked out over a sea of

faces and began to feel frightened. He asked the Holy Ghost to lead his words. Once the singing began, Sammy forgot everything except the love of God. His plain face radiated Christ's love, and it was clear he had a message for the student body.

At the conclusion of the meeting, crowds of students knelt with Sammy in prayer.

Afterwards, Dr. Reade wrote about the message, "I was so surprised at the freshness and force of Sammy's thoughts. He spoke for forty minutes in a quiet, yet earnest style, simple and natural as a child. All who had honest hearts to receive the truth profited from his words."

The next morning at breakfast, everyone was discussing the revival meetings. Aman sat quietly as student after student congratulated Sammy. Some of them said he was a "blessing to their souls." Others called him "an angel in ebony" or "a messenger of God." Sammy was embarrassed at the many compliments and praises. He kept repeating in protest, "I wish you would give praise to Jesus and not to me."

After the meal, Sammy left Aman in the dining hall and headed to attend services at the Berry Street Church. A church family invited Sammy to dinner in their home, so he didn't return to the campus in time to pick up his sack lunch.

Usually Sammy and Aman ate their sack lunches together on Sunday evening. The dining hall was closed to give the cooks some time off. This Sunday, when Sammy knocked at Aman's door, there was no answer. He wondered, *Where is Aman?* Because he didn't show up, Sammy went to the revival service with Eddie. The day flew past in a whirlwind of activities.

Monday morning Sammy continued to glow with the wonders of the revival and God's blessings. He knocked on Aman's door and called out, "Ready for breakfast?"

Aman opened his door and said, "Well, if the great angel in ebony hasn't come for me!" He acted surprised to see Sammy.

"I always come for you. What do you mean?"

"I thought God's great messenger would be too busy to bother with me," Aman said with a forced smile.

"You must be joking," Sammy said. He didn't understand the tension in Aman's voice and actions. It puzzled him, but he studied as usual.

That afternoon, Dr. Macbeth smiled and said, "Now is the time for the spelling contest. We shall see who wins this prize." She held up a box wrapped in flowery paper and ribbon.

Aman took the first word and spelled it correctly. Then Sammy spelled his word correctly. Then Dr. Macbeth gave another word to Aman. "Correct." And again to Sammy, "Correct." Aman spelled with confidence, and it was easy to see he knew every word.

"Correct," Dr. Macbeth said each time. Finally she turned to Sammy and said, "Either."

Sammy remembered the rule they had learned, *I before E except after C.*

"Hum," he said, "I-E-T-H-E-R."

Suddenly Aman began to laugh, and Dr. Macbeth handed him the prize. He quickly unwrapped the package and saw a wood carving of a monkey. He was outraged and said, "You call me a monkey? There is your monkey." Aman pointed to Sammy. "None of you really knows him, and you think that he is good!"

"You don't?" Dr. Macbeth asked. "What has he done, Aman?"

"Last week, Sammy called me a thief for suggesting that we open the window of this room and get our spelling books. Then he, himself, opened the window, got his spelling book, and then studied all weekend to win this contest. He always wants to outshine me!"

"Sammy!" Dr. Macbeth said. "Did you call Aman a thief?"

"No, Dr. Macbeth. I said that we should not open the window like thieves."

"And you should not," Dr. Macbeth agreed. "We lock the door so no one should come in, but did you, Sammy?"

"Yes, Dr. Macbeth."

"Why?"

Sammy said, "I changed my mind. I decided it wasn't so bad to open the window just to get our spelling books."

"So it is true that you studied in secret all weekend so you could win the contest over Aman!" Dr. Macbeth shot Sammy a disappointed look.

"I was at the revival this weekend. I meant to get with Aman and study for the spelling contest, but he wasn't in his room when I knocked; anyway there wasn't time to study." Sammy felt upset because the more he defended himself, the worse he sounded.

Aman smirked, "See Dr. Macbeth. See how white and innocent he acts, like a lily. The students call him an angel in ebony. They don't know how he sneaks to outshine me, the son of a Bible woman."

Dr. Macbeth's mouth fell open in surprise. "I think we need to have a time of prayer." Immediately she knelt and waited for both young men to kneel. All three of them knelt in silence for a long time. Dr. Macbeth prayed, asking the Holy Ghost to work in the hearts of her students. Both students prayed.

Then Sammy stood and clasped Aman's hands. "Dear friend, I'm sorry I offended you. Forgive me. I do not wish to outshine you or anyone. Really."

Dr. Macbeth touched Aman. "What do you have to say? Are you sorry that you were jealous of Sammy?"

Aman's head dropped. "I am very sorry I made the heavenly angels weep."

When the warm spring weather arrived, Dr. Macbeth put on a white dress and went to her classroom. Sammy was seated in the room when she arrived. He looked up and appeared surprised at her appearance. He began to laugh aloud and asked, "Why do you folks in this country wear clothes all summer?" His question contained no suggestion of rudeness, but merely highlighted the difference between the customs of America and Africa.

In spite of Sammy's odd questions and ways, he was well treated and greatly respected. Later, President Reade wrote about Sammy as the first black person at

Taylor. "I wish to say here to the honor of the faculty and students of the university, if Sammy had been the president's son, he could not have been treated with greater courtesy. He was loved and respected by all."

nine

During his first year at Taylor, Samuel Morris arrived after the leaves had fallen. He was totally unprepared for the array of color from the trees in the next autumn. He had lived in the tropics, which is a land of perpetual summer.

"God is surely good to you folks in Indiana," Sammy said. "In Africa, our leaves are always green."

Sammy loved to smell the flowers around the university. In Liberia they had beautiful flowers, but they lacked the scents of the flowers in America. As he buried his nose in the flowers, he said, "This must be how heaven smells."

As was common with many other Christian men and women who have left behind what the poet Longfellow called "footprints on the sands of time," Sammy was a great lover of nature. He loved the outdoors and often took walks to drink in the beauty of the land. The singing of the birds and fragrance of the flowers filled Sammy with joy.

The first snow that fell after Sammy came to America happened to be masses of large, icy flakes. It started to fall during the night and was still falling when Sammy woke up in the morning. He looked out the window. Everything was covered with a sparkling white blanket. Sammy was surprised and awestruck. He had never seen snow or heard of it.

Like the Israelites who, when God provided new food and scattered it across the ground of Israel like frost, shouted in amazement, "Manna! Manna! What is it?" Sammy rushed out into the snow and gathered up a handful. "These must be messages from heaven to us," he said. "If I could only read them, what a wonderful story they would tell us! Earth has nothing half so beautiful. God alone has such a pattern." Sammy was reminded of the words in Job 38:22: "Have you entered into the treasures of the snow?"

As Sammy spoke, his warm hand melted the snow it held. "Where did it go?" asked an astonished Sammy. "It left this water in my hand!" He shook his head in wonder. "The Lord is sure good to you folks in Indiana!" His eyes filled with tears, then he raised his hands and prayed to his Father to teach him all about these beautiful messages from heaven. As he finished his prayer, he said, "A year here is worth a lifetime in Africa."

Sammy's body was not used to the cold climate. That winter his ears were affected by the freezing temperatures. He was in great pain. As was his custom, he talked to his Father about it. The pain left him, and he went about his busy schedule. The tortures Sammy had endured in Africa while serving as a slave for the Grebos and the severe hardships he had suffered aboard the ship had greatly weakened his frail body. The long, cold winters were unnatural for someone like Sammy, who grew up in the tropics.

Sammy became very involved with the churches in the area. He was an active member of the Berry Street Methodist Episcopal Church and continued to attend services at the Methodist Episcopal Church on East Wayne Street.

Sammy's days were filled with study, worship, and fellowship. He continued to study with Aman, learning English, basic skills, and Bible with the help of tutors. Aman's goal was to return to his homeland of Armenia and help his mother preach the gospel there. Sammy often shared with Aman his own dream to return to Liberia and share the gospel with his people. Sammy would also take walks with his university friends. Together they would talk of their plans for their lives. Sammy would talk of Liberia.

"When I go back," he would say, "I will gather the children together. We will sit in a circle on the sand. I will tell them all about Jesus." His face warmed at the thought. "I know they will go into the forest to pray. Then they will have joy."

Sammy had a heart for the children of his people. He remembered the hardships of his own childhood and the uncertainty of his life then. He was ever filled with joy that God had ransomed the young prince Kaboo. He wanted other children to know the same glorious love.

One day Sammy was talking with Dr. Reade about his teachers. He laughed and said, "I don't think I shall

149

love my teachers in heaven any better than I love you, Dr. Stemen, Dr. Macbeth, and Miss Husted, but I shall learn faster there; I shall not be so dumb."

On another occasion, Sammy and Dr. Reade prepared to walk into the dining room for Thanksgiving. It marked the second such holiday for Sammy and he mentioned his delight with the fall colors. Above the clatter of the dishes, Dr. Reade listened. He also asked questions like, "Sammy, which country do you like the best, Africa or America?"

Instead of answering the question, Sammy turned around with another question. "Dr. Reade, which do you like best, roast turkey or raw monkey?"

"Why, Sammy, you didn't eat monkeys, did you?" Dr. Reade looked a bit surprised.

"Oh, yes, I ate monkeys and ate them raw."

Dr. Reade decided to change the topic of conversation. "Does it bother you to be the only black person in our school?"

"No, sir," Sammy answered. "When I nicked off a small piece of skin and found I was white underneath the black, I put black ink over it. I was afraid there might be a white spot left on my skin when it healed."

Dr. Reade laughed, "I'm glad we have made you feel right at home!"

Sammy's face turned serious and he said, "I'm glad that I'm black. When I return home and preach to my own people, they will listen." It wasn't often that Sammy talked to Dr. Reade about his dreams of returning home to his people. Sometimes he felt like his dream would be impossible to achieve.

"I have a favor to ask you, Sammy," the president began. "Whenever I've asked before, you've refused to allow your photograph to be taken. I'm writing your story for a church paper, and I really need a picture of you. Will you let us take your photo?"

Sammy looked at his friend and said, "It is just that I am so ugly. I want people to see Jesus and not me."

With more encouragement from the president, Sammy finally agreed to have his photo taken.

After their plates of turkey arrived, there was a general lull in the conversation. Dr. Reade turned to Sammy and asked, "How do you like our snow?"

Sammy laughed, "Do you know that we have no word for snow in the Nigrite language? I was so amazed when I looked out of my room one morning and saw it. I ran outside and gathered a handful of snow."

He continued, "When the snow melted, I said, 'Where did it go? It has left only a few drops of water!' If I could understand, Dr. Reade, I think God sends us messages from heaven in the snow."

Dr. Reade agreed. "We do need to thank our Maker for 'all things bright and beautiful,' as the song says."

"You know," Sammy reflected, "a year here is worth a lifetime in Africa."

With happy feelings, Sammy settled down to begin eating his Thanksgiving dinner. It was such a feast!

"There is another thing that I need to discuss with you, Sammy," Dr. Reade began as he sank his fork into the pumpkin pie. "We need to talk about the city revival."

151

"What revival?" Sammy asked. He loved preaching.

"This revival is for everyone in Fort Wayne. The only building that will be large enough for it is the roller skating rink on West Main Street. The meetings will be held there, though it will be cold, I know."

"What can I do to help?" Sammy asked.

"We want you to sit on the platform and pray. Your very presence with us will count for God."

Sammy agreed to the assignment, but continued to ask a lot of questions about the roller rink. He had never heard of roller skating. After hearing a description of it, Sammy said, "I'd like to try it one day."

"Well, don't bite off more than you can chew," the president cautioned. "If you didn't learn as a child, you could get hurt trying it now."

Sammy laughed, "There is a saying, 'Be sure to keep an eye out for what you can swallow, and also for what can swallow you.' "

Dr. Reade laughed. "That's exactly what I meant! Sammy, you always amaze me."

Sammy attended the revival meetings at the old skating rink. Every night he was on the platform. When the hymns were sung, Sammy's voice rang out with singular joy. He was always available, ready to pray with anyone in need.

One of the people who attended these meetings described Sammy Morris with these words: "His honest black face was a benediction; his simple heart yearning

152

for truth was an inspiration to the minister to do his best to tell the gospel story."

All racial and economic barriers fell wherever Sammy was; he prayed for white, black, rich, or poor. The results were always the same. People were touched by God.

The winter of 1892 to 1893 in Indiana was exceptionally cold. During January, Sammy caught a severe cold, but he didn't stay home. Instead, he attended every revival service—even when the temperature dipped to twenty degrees below zero and the night was dark and stormy.

Nothing would stop the young man from attending all the church meetings during the week. He was always there to sing and pray, to bask in the presence of his Lord. During the meetings, Sammy struggled to smother his coughing. The ministers admired his simple faith in Christ.

At the final meeting, the ministers asked Sammy to lead the congregation in singing the hymn, "Tell Me the Old, Old Story of Jesus and His Love." No one forgot the light on Sammy's face while he sang the song. He was filled with the love of the Holy Ghost, and many awoke to Christ's call on their lives as a result.

Sammy's cold worsened, but he continued his studies. His digestive system developed problems with the steady diet of American food. One day when Sammy discovered a Bible verse about fasting, he began to abstain from foods. From Thursday evening until Saturday morning, he would never take a morsel of food nor a drop of water, yet his work went on and he seemed so cheerful and happy that no one knew about his fasting but those who missed him from the dining room table.

Sammy's physical condition weakened, but he kept silent about it to the school officials and acted as though nothing was wrong with him. He continued attending classes until his strength failed and finally he admitted that he was gravely ill.

"Why didn't you tell us sooner?" Dr. Macbeth admonished.

When he heard about Sammy's condition, Dr. C. B. Stemen had his young friend admitted to the hospital immediately. Aman went to St. Joseph's Hospital with Sammy. The Armenian student was impressed with the concern that everyone showed Sammy.

Sammy said, "When I froze my ears last winter, they hurt me very much. I asked my Father about it, and He healed me right away. Now, I ask Him to be healed and He does not do it. I don't understand it."

For weeks, Sammy was in the hospital with pneumonia. Fellow students and faculty continued to visit their beloved Sammy. One day as some of his friends gathered in his hospital room, they noticed the puzzled look in Sammy's face was gone. His face was relaxed and covered with a glowing peace.

"I understand now why my Father has not healed me. He showed me that I have finished my work here on earth. I have done all that I was meant to do. It is time for me to go and be with Him. I saw the angels! They will be coming for me soon! The light my Father in heaven sent to save me when I was hanging helpless on that cross in Africa was for a purpose. Now my work here on earth has been finished."

Dr. Reade came to sit with him. As Sammy related his latest conversation with his Father, Dr. Reade protested.

"But what about going back to Africa? What about your work with the children?"

Sammy smiled at his friend. "It is not my work, Dr. Reade. It is Christ's work. I have finished my job. He must choose his own workers. Others can do the work in Africa better."

Dr. Reade's eyes brimmed with tears. "But Sammy" His voice broke.

"I am so happy to be going home!" exclaimed Sammy.

The college president gazed at the young man who did not once complain of his suffering. "Sammy, are you afraid of death?"

Sammy laughed and shook his head. "How can I fear death? I have Jesus! Death is my friend!"

What a contrast to the terror death held for the young Kaboo who lay dying in Africa five years before! Kaboo had learned that death was the gateway to life. He understood that life was a bright eternal river that flowed from the throne of his Father.

Dr. Reade remembered when Sammy had come to him one day, laughing. He remembered his words: "Dr. Reade, I doubt I could possibly love my teachers in heaven more than I love you, and Dr. Macbeth, and the rest of my teachers here." His eyes had twinkled in

155

merriment. "But in heaven, I will not be so slow a student. I will be a fast learner there!"

The college president left Sammy to rest. He wondered if Sammy was right about dying. Everyone else seemed to think he would recover.

On May 12, 1893, Sammy stood at the window of his hospital room. It was a sunny spring day. He was watching Dr. Stemen, who lived across the street from the hospital, mow his lawn.

"Dr. Stemen!" called Sammy from his window. "Don't work too hard!"

Dr. Stemen waved to his friend. Sammy returned to his chair.

In a matter of minutes, Sister Helen from the hospital frantically summoned Dr. Stemen to Sammy's room. She couldn't get her patient to respond.

Dr. Stemen took the ebony arm in his hand and felt for a pulse. There was none. He looked at Sammy's face. It radiated joyful peace.

"He's gone," said the doctor softly.

In Sammy's lap rested a hymnbook opened to his favorite hymn:

> *Fade, fade, each earthly joy.*
> *Jesus is mine,*
> *Break every tender tie,*
> *Jesus is mine!*

Perhaps, echoing in the walls of that room were words from Sammy's favorite chapter in Scripture: "Let

156

not your heart be troubled: ye believe in God, believe also in me. In my Father's house are many mansions: if it were not so, I would have told you. I go to prepare a place for you. And if I go and prepare a place for you, I will come again, and receive you unto myself; that where I am, there ye may be also" (John 14:1-3). Sammy was in his Father's house!

The news of Samuel Morris's death swept across the university campus, dealing every heart a jolting blow. How could this be? He was so young, so full of promise. What a mighty ministry he was going to have! Why did the Lord allow him to die? What about the children in Liberia? What about the hundreds of people in the surrounding community who had come to love Sammy?

The university had been preparing for the laying of the cornerstone for its new home in Upland, Indiana. The railroads were preparing to run excursion trains for the event. Samuel Morris was to have spoken and sung. The school was planning on Sammy to be the main attraction for the dedication. His sudden death plunged the entire community into profound grief. Every heart wondered at God's will in taking away a life so young and full of promise. Was all of Sammy's faith to end in a cloud of doubt?

At the time of Sammy's death, Dr. Reade was in Upland attending to details about the university's upcoming move. When Dr. Reade left Fort Wayne, he didn't realize that Sammy's illness had reached a critical point. When he received the news about Sammy's death, he felt as if someone had struck him with a crushing blow.

He wept and sobbed like a little child. Later he wrote of his feelings at that time: "Samuel Morris was dead; the wonderful and loving soul, whose future was all bright with the promise of hope, whose life had been a benediction to Taylor University." The grief and pain that throbbed in his heart was something he could not express. When Dr. Reade returned to the campus, he felt that Sammy's death left a vacant place in the school.

The entire student body felt Sammy's loss. There was gloom and depression in the atmosphere of the school rooms at the report that Sammy was dead. His voice, which echoed in prayers in the silent hours of the night, was to be heard no more. His solemn and inspiring figure, which had awakened slumbering souls to the love and goodness of God, was to be seen no longer in their presence. Gone was the apostle of simple faith, the angel of ebony, the embodiment of childlike humility.

The students wanted to offer Sammy their last tribute of love so they took turns at night watching around the casket, which lay in the college chapel. Face to face with the lifeless remains of someone they had learned to love, these students started to think about the meaning of his short life.

On the day of his funeral, ten students, among them Sammy's good friends Aman and Eddie, carried the coffin the ten blocks to the Berry Street Methodist Episcopal Church. The street was lined on both sides with students, faculty members, and churchgoers.

Everyone removed their hats as the body of Samuel Morris was carried to the church. Many were unable to get into the church service, but they waited outside and attended the graveside ceremony at Lindewood Cemetery. Mourners from all over the city came to say farewell to Samuel Morris.

The graveside ceremony was the largest ever seen in Fort Wayne, but as was the rule of that day, the cemetery was divided into two sections: one for white people and one for black people. The young man who had been a Grebo slave was buried with slaves and descendants of slaves in America.

Dr. Macbeth contributed the money for the tombstone, which read:

Samuel Morris—1873-1893
Prince Kaboo
Native of West Africa
Exponent of the Spirit-Filled Life

Dr. Reade said, "Samuel Morris was a divinely sent messenger of God to Taylor University. He came to prepare himself, but his coming prepared the university for a missionary training program."

After the funeral, the college students gathered in a prayer meeting. They talked together of their beloved friend. Eddie rose and said, "I feel impressed I must go to Africa in Sammy's place. I pray that as his work has fallen on me, so the mantle of his faith may likewise fall upon me." Two other students also dedicated their lives to missions that night.

After overcoming the initial shock of Sammy's

159

death, his friends began to realize the greater vision that God had had for his young life. God's measurement of life is so different from the way people measure. It's not the length of a life that matters. Rather it is whether or not the life was lived wholeheartedly for the Lord. Sammy's simple faith in his Father caused others to be drawn to the Lord. His fervent prayers sparked intercession in those who heard him pray. His gentleness and willingness to serve humbled those around him, spurring them to be servants as well.

Sammy always pointed people to Jesus. When his reputation as a servant of the Lord spread, many people wrote to Taylor University requesting photographs of the inspiring young man. Sammy's reaction could be the theme of his life: "How I wish I could send them a picture of Jesus!"

In a way, Sammy's cry was answered. Because of his humility, his faith, and his love, his life was indeed a picture of Jesus. When God reached out to a young boy dying on a cross in Africa, it was the beginning of a journey that would ultimately affect people around the world. What a testimony to the love and grace of God! Prince Kaboo could have simply died of his wounds, alone and unknown. But God had a plan for his young life. He called him out of his misery and showered him with love.

Sammy's story is a miracle, a wonder. But it is a wonder and a marvel that any of us are saved. It is a miracle of grace when we hear the voice of God in His gospel and follow that voice, set free from the clutching jungle of sin and the evil chieftain of the kingdom of darkness, Satan.

Prince Kaboo was torn from his family. He lost his earthly father. But God reached down and became a Father to him, a Father who would never leave or forsake His child. This wonderful Savior redeemed the pawn from death. And Sammy's response to such love provided a channel of giving that helped to change the lives of countless others.

What did Sammy know that resulted in such far-reaching fruitfulness? He knew how much God loved the world. And he was fully convinced of the love of God for one boy named Kaboo.

ten

B ecause Sammy lived and died a Spirit-filled life, many lives were changed. Aman and many other students who knew Sammy dedicated their lives to following the guidance of the Holy Ghost.

The small church on Berry Street where Sammy worshiped in Fort Wayne continued to grow in membership. The following winter, the church increased until there were so many new members that the church had to expand with a new building.

The Samuel Morris Faith Fund has helped hundreds of students prepare for the mission field. As Dr. Reade wrote about the Faith Fund, "It still lives and has never been exhausted. It has never at any time had fifty dollars to its credit, for the contributions by which it has been fed have been small, and as soon as received were placed to the credit of some indigent student, but there has been—Glory to God!—there has always been a 'little oil in the vase and a little meal in the barrel.'

"The contributions to this faith fund have come to us by mail in amounts varying from one dollar to one hundred dollars, and from every state in the Union and from Canada. We have received two gifts of one hundred dollars each: one from the state of New Jersey, and one from the far-off Sweden."

When Sammy died, he only possessed the meager sum of eight dollars. But the life he lived and his spiritual lessons are an inheritance that are more valuable than any material possessions. His brief biography written by Dr. Reade and sold for ten cents each provided Taylor University with twenty thousand dollars at a time when it was desperately needed.

During the fall of 1893, Taylor University was moved to Upland, Indiana. School authorities were anxious to make the move because of the indebtedness of the school in Fort Wayne and the gift of land and a bonus of ten thousand dollars.

But the first year in Upland proved difficult. A nationwide financial panic threatened the school with bankruptcy. In the dead of winter, the crisis became so acute that the school lacked coal and other necessities. Many students threatened to leave the school. Some professors had not received their salary for months.

Many financial supporters of the school became discouraged and began to think the days of the school were numbered. But the school was saved through the heroic efforts of the faculty and some of the students. These people believed in the mission of the school and God's directing guidance. Dr. Reade wrote a small sketch of Samuel Morris's life, which reached a circulation of two hundred thousand copies.

Years later Dr. Burt W. Ayres, a past vice president of Taylor University, described how that small booklet of Dr. Reade's transformed lives and changed the direction of Taylor University: "In the early years of my connection with Taylor University, I was impressed with the wonderful influence of the life of Samuel Morris.

"Each fall many of the new students, in giving their religious experiences, would speak of having read the booklet on the life of Sammy Morris written by President Reade and tell how it was through that that they had been influenced to come to Taylor. They spoke of the great blessing received from reading this brief account of his life.

"In those days, gifts to the school were usually not in what we now call large sums, but many who sent in money were moved to do so by the story of this wonderful life. The booklet was translated into a number of other languages in European countries and bore fruit, both material and spiritual.

"I distinctly remember checks as large as fifty and one hundred dollars—very large gifts in those days—coming from people in Norway and Sweden. Not only did this little book bring students and gifts of money, but the large sale of the book brought in considerable money, which was used to help educate worthy students who had no money and could not have remained in school but for these gifts and the employment given them by the school.

"Formerly ministers would order these little books by the hundred and distribute them free or sell them to their people when preparing for a revival, and they frequently wrote to the school, telling them of the wonderful spiritual uplift received.

"Many factors have entered into the life of Taylor University without anyone of which, humanly speaking, the school must have failed in the crucial decade just following the moving of the school to Upland. I believe the very life of the school depended upon the dynamic of this Spirit-filled life, preserved and released to the reading religious world by the pen of Thaddeus C. Reade."

The phenomenal sales of the booklet were not confined to America alone. It has been translated into different European languages and into Indian dialects, broadening its influence. The story of Samuel Morris's life brought Taylor University to the eyes of the world. It is not strange that gifts came from as far as Sweden and that many foreign students turned their attention to Upland, Indiana, for their American education.

Another book on Samuel Morris was written by a former student of Taylor University, Mr. Lindley J. Baldwin. He had known Sammy personally and heard of his wonderful experiences firsthand. Nearly half a century after Sammy died, Mr. Baldwin wrote Sammy's story.

After Mr. Baldwin completed his manuscript, he read it to Dr. Harriet Macbeth, who as a young woman had been Sammy's teacher. At the time she was nearly blind and had been bedridden for weeks. The reading was accompanied by yet another miracle, for Dr. Macbeth was able to rise immediately from her sickbed, restored in health and strength.

Once Mr. Baldwin was staying with a Roman

Catholic family, the Shaffers, who noticed a copy of a booklet about Sammy Morris sticking out of Mr. Baldwin's pocket. The booklet led Mr. Baldwin into a discussion over the supper table.

Nearby was a Protestant church where a meeting was being held that evening. It was bitterly cold and the heater for the building had failed. Mr. Baldwin's friends invited the whole congregation to their house. The Shaffers suggested that the story of Sammy Morris should be read.

Here's how Mr. Baldwin described the results of the reading of Sammy's story: "If Sammy had been present in person, the effect could not have been more wonderful. One after another prayed as if his life depended upon it. One of the Shaffer boys cried out, 'Brethren, that light from Africa is in our midst. Let us keep it burning!'"

Everyone in the house felt the presence of the Holy Ghost that night. When the time came for them to separate and go to their various homes, they had had an experience that none of them ever forgot. Later one member of the Shaffer family attended Taylor University.

Throughout the years, multitudes of students yielded their lives to God when they heard Sammy's story. Eventually, Taylor University Bible School was established in Africa. In this training center, Africans could be trained as teachers and evangelists without having to travel so far from their homes.

One tribute Taylor University paid to Samuel Morris was to name a dormitory after him in 1908. In 1958, a second men's dorm replaced Samuel Morris Hall, but it was given the same name so that students could be constantly reminded of Sammy's life. Presently, a third building to bear Morris's name is scheduled for construction on the Taylor University campus.

Recently, three statues of Sammy Morris were dedicated at Taylor University. These statues, which appear in front of the Communications Art building, picture Sammy in three different situations: "Escaping His Captors," "The Moment of Revelation," and "The Taylor Student Filled with the Holy Ghost."

But the story of Sammy's life is more about the changes it brought to others than honors now given in his memory. In his booklet about Sammy, Dr. Thaddeus C. Reade explained: "In writing this little sketch, my only desire is that the people may know what wonders our God can do when He finds a willing, obedient, confiding subject through whom and in whom to work.

"Most of us, I fear, have gone too far away from the simple faith of childhood, and God cannot do mighty works in us because of our unbelief. The faith of Sammy Morris never wavered and never questioned; hence God, who chooses the weak things to confound the mighty, put His power upon him.

"I suppose that Mary of Bethany never dreamed of acquiring an immortal name; she scarcely knew the meaning of such a thing. Her only ambition was to be known and loved by a little circle of friends about her humble home, and to enjoy the approval of the Master, who came and called on her. But because Mary anointed the feet of Jesus with costly nard and bathed them with her grateful tears and wiped them with her hair, her name was immortal. 'Verily, I say until you, whereso-ever this gospel shall be preached, in the whole world, that also which this woman hath done, shall be spoken of as a memorial of her.' She probably had not the faintest idea of the far-reaching meaning of His words, but they teach us to honor all good works and perpetuate every noble example.

"If the subject of this sketch were alive and should be made acquainted with my purpose to publish to the world the simple story of his life, he would stare in blank amazement at the announcement. He would turn his honest, black face to mine, and after a few moments of thoughtful silence, he would slowly shake his head, and raising his great eyes upward, he would say: 'No, no, Mr. Reade; tell them not about poor Sammy Morris, but about Jesus. Tell them about the Holy Ghost. . . .'

"To me this simple black boy was a daily wonder, a visible miracle of the utmost grace of God. . . . I trust that in the story of his life he may prove a blessing to thousands of others as he has been to me and hundreds of others while living."

In New York, several years after Sammy's death, the captain of a tramp vessel knocked on Stephen Merritt's door.

"Excuse me, sir," he said. "I'm a friend of Samuel Morris. My crew and I are anxious to hear about him. Can you tell me, is he well? How is he doing?"

Stephen Merritt looked into the grizzly face of the old captain. There was so much to tell of Sammy. Where to begin? Merritt smiled and said, "He set Taylor

University on fire with the Holy Ghost."

"Like he did my ship!" The captain laughed delight-edly. "Where is he now?"

"With Jesus. He never reached twenty-one years of age, but dozens of Taylor students have taken his place on the mission field."

The captain was stunned with the news. "He offered the first prayer on my ship. My men are waiting to find out what happened. I'm so sorry he is dead." Then the captain fell silent. Overwhelmed with grief, he couldn't speak.

Stephen sat with him in the silence, sharing his grief. When at last he spoke, the captain testified to the wonderful influence Sammy had had on the entire crew. "My men are from all parts of the world. We're all dif-ferent, all from different cultures. Sammy did the impossible. Through his prayers, his singing, his way of living, he made us one. Where there was hate and divi-sion, there is now unity. We are like a family now."

Stephen Merritt said, "Although Sammy is dead, he still speaks to us through the story of his life." Together they bowed their heads and Dr. Merritt prayed, "Oh, God, I pray the Holy Ghost will touch young people every day to believe—as Sammy Morris believed. Amen."

Just as the lives of the captain and his men were for-ever changed by God through Sammy, Stephen Merritt's life was changed as well. He resolutely endeavored to walk with the Holy Ghost, following His lead. His min-istry exploded with fruitfulness. Thousands of people came to Christ through his ministry.

Although Sammy had been buried in the part of the cemetery reserved for African Americans, because he had pulled down barriers between the races, his grave was moved to link the two sections, black and white, together. Thirty-five years after his death, a monument was erected to honor him. These words were carved in it:

Samuel Morris, 1873-1893
Prince Kaboo
Native of West Africa
Famous Christian Mystic
Apostle of Simple Faith
Exponent of the Spirit-filled Life
Student at Taylor University 1892-93
Fort Wayne, now located at Upland,
Indiana. The story of his life
a vital contribution to the
development of Taylor University
* * *

The erection of this memorial was sponsored by the 1928 class of Taylor University, and funds were contributed by Fort Wayne citizens.

Sammy's grave is visited more often by more people than any other grave in the cemetery. People have gone there and been drawn to pray and seek the Lord. Even in death, Samuel Morris still points people to Christ.

One woman who had lost her health, her husband, and her savings was unable to find work. At her wit's end, she gathered wildflowers for her husband's tomb and sank down on the ground in a state of complete collapse.

Then she noticed a group of people gathering at the grave of Samuel Morris. As she heard these people speaking about Sammy, she thought, *If the Lord could use him when he had nothing, He can save me.* She prayed. She seemed to hear Sammy's voice saying, "Pray to my Father; He will save you. He will send the Holy Ghost to lead you." She felt the presence of the Spirit of God and her prayers were answered.

The widow joined the Salvation Army. Since that time, when she encounters an especially hard and cynical person to deal with, she has taken that person to Sammy's grave and prayed. Lives have been transformed. The same benediction of God has been felt at Sammy's grave by thousands of others who have been converted there or endowed with a fresh measure of spiritual vision and hope.

In 1896, Dr. Reade published a revised booklet about Sammy's life. As word got out that he was working on the booklet, he began receiving letters from Sammy's classmates and acquaintances who wanted to share their experiences with Sammy. One of those letters came from Mrs. S. F. Beiderwell, who with her husband attended Taylor while Sammy was a student. Mrs. Beiderwell wrote to Dr. Reade from Rolla, Missouri, where here husband was preaching:

Dear Doctor Reade:
Mr. Beiderwell and I are both very glad you are

171

going to revise the "Life of Sammy Morris." As soon as I read the book, I remarked it was a pity it was so brief, as there were so many more valuable facts connected with his life which ought to be published. We that knew the faith and piety of Sammy can say as the Sheban Queen did, "The half had not been told me."

Many times Mr. Beiderwell and I have been led to consecrate our lives more fully to God through the influence of this boy. He surely was a missionary to all his fellow students at Taylor University. Whenever he would be at our home in the evening, he would always request us to have family worship with him before he would go, and he invariably wished Mr. Beiderwell to read him the 14th chapter of St. John. At times he wanted us to join him in singing his favorite hymn, "Behold the Bridegroom."

You, no doubt, remember the time I was hearing Sammy and Jimmie Thompson recite a lesson in parsing in your office. Sammy was parsing the word heaven and said it was a proper noun, as there was only one heaven.

When Dr. Reade released the revised booklet about Sammy Morris's life, he observed: "I, too, with the multitudes of weeping hearts, have asked over and over again, 'Why, why, why?' It may not be for us to know all the secrets of God's mysterious ways at present. We are still in the flesh and bound by the limits of the finite. If the dear Lord would draw aside the misty veil that separates us from the future, we might understand it better.

"Samuel Morris was a divinely sent messenger of God to touch Taylor University. He thought he was coming over to prepare himself for his mission in the world —he was coming over to this country to prepare Taylor University for her mission in this world. She was ready for his message, and it lifted her to a new realm. She got a vision of the world's needs. It was no longer local, neither national, but worldwide. . . . Since then the students have been going to the ends of the world."

The experience of Sammy Morris is one of the most wonderful stories in the almost two-thousand-year history of the Christian Church. We know enough about his short life to say with certainty that it was not wasted. Countless men, women, boys, and girls have been drawn nearer to God through the life and witness of this African boy.

Samuel Morris never reached the age of twenty-one, and he lived but a scant five years after coming out of the jungles of Africa. Yet in that short time—about the equivalent to our high school years—his name became known around the world. Few religious leaders of his time period had greater influence with missionaries of various church denominations.

But his influence has been producing results in increasing volumes for many decades. Before Sammy came to Taylor, it was a college without a special missionary vision or purpose. After his death, three Taylor University students went out as missionaries because of

173

the influence Sammy had on their lives. Seven students—more than twice as many as the original group—went out from the university as missionaries a short time later.

Soon Taylor became known as a place where many students prepared for missionary service in Africa. Several missionaries from Taylor were buried on African soil—Oliver Moody, Susan Talbot Wengatz, and John C. Overshire.

Sammy's impact on Taylor University is still felt. Taylor is a thriving college that continues to send out students as missionaries across the globe.

The legacy of Samuel Morris—Prince Kaboo—lives on. His testimony, his childlike faith, inspire people to this day. Sammy would be the first to say that it is not his personality that can so engage the human spirit, rather it is the Holy Ghost of God working through him. It is a testimony to what God can do with the life of one who follows Jesus wholeheartedly.

For Additional Reading

Many books have been written about Samuel Morris since Dr. Reade first produced his little booklet. While not all of these books are currently in print, most of them can be obtained through public libraries.

African Prince; The True Story of Samuel Morris (Prince Kaboo). United Missionary Society, 1958.

Baez, Kjersti Hoff. *The Life of Samuel Morris*. Barbour Books, 1993.

Baldwin, Lindley J. *Samuel Morris*. Bethany House Publishers, 1942.

Evans, A. R. *Sammy Morris*. Zondervan Publishing House, 1958.

Konkle, Wilbur. *Jungle Gold; The Amazing Story of Sammy Morris and True Stories on African Life*. Pillar of Fire Press, 1966.

Masa, Jorge O. *The Angel in Ebony, or, The Life and Message of Sammy Morris*. Taylor University Press, 1928.

Reade, Thaddeus C. *Samuel Morris (Prince Kaboo)*. Taylor University Press, 1921.

Stocker, Fern Neal. *Sammy Morris*. Moody Press, 1986.

Reed, D. E. *Samuel Morris: A Spirit-filled Life*. Pentecostal Publishing Company, 1908.

Wengatz, John C. *Sammy Morris: The Spirit-filled Life*. Taylor University Press, 1954.

Index